Cultivate Cannabis Confidence

A Beginner's Guide to Successful Weed Growth

Jessica Bennett

Table of Contents

INTRODUCTION

"Cultivate Cannabis Confidence: A Beginner's Guide to Successful Weed Growth" is a comprehensive e-book designed to empower individuals new to cannabis cultivation with the knowledge and skills needed to embark on a successful journey into growing their marijuana plants. As the societal perspective on cannabis undergoes a transformative shift, more people are exploring the possibilities of cultivating their supply for personal use. This e-book is a valuable resource for beginners, providing a solid foundation to navigate the complex world of cannabis cultivation.

The e-book begins by demystifying the process of growing cannabis, breaking the essentials into easily understandable chapters. From selecting suitable strains and germinating seeds to creating an optimal growing environment, readers are guided through each stage of the cultivation process. The content is presented in a beginner-friendly manner, ensuring that even those with no experience in gardening or horticulture can grasp the fundamentals.

One of the standout features of "Cultivate Cannabis Confidence" is its emphasis on building a solid foundation in cannabis knowledge. Readers learn how to grow their plants successfully and gain insights into the anatomy of the cannabis plant, the intricacies of different strains, and the significance of environmental factors in cultivation. The e-book goes beyond a mere step-by-step guide, fostering a deeper understanding of the plant and the cultivation process.

In addition to technical guidance, the e-book addresses common challenges beginners face and provides troubleshooting tips to overcome potential hurdles. Whether pest management, nutrient deficiencies, or environmental concerns, readers will find practical solutions to ensure a thriving cannabis garden.

"Cultivate Cannabis Confidence" stands out as an empowering and informative resource, equipping beginners with the confidence and knowledge needed to cultivate high-quality cannabis at home. As cannabis cultivation becomes more mainstream, this e-book serves as a guiding light for those eager to embark on a successful and rewarding journey into the world of weed cultivation.

CHAPTER I

Understanding Cannabis Plants

Anatomy of the Cannabis Plant

The anatomy of the cannabis plant is a complex and fascinating subject, offering insight into the intricacies of a species cultivated and revered for its diverse uses for centuries. At its core, the cannabis plant, scientifically known as Cannabis sativa, is a dioecious, flowering herb that belongs to the Cannabaceae family. Understanding its anatomy is pivotal for anyone involved in cannabis cultivation, from hobbyists to commercial growers.

The cannabis plant exhibits a distinctive morphology, characterized by various structures and components contributing to its overall form and function. At the foundation of every cannabis plant is the root system, hidden beneath the soil. Roots serve as the anchor, providing stability and absorbing water and nutrients essential for the plant's growth. The root system consists of primary and secondary roots, each crucial in sustaining the plant's overall health and vitality.

Above the ground, the cannabis plant features a robust stem, supporting the plant's structure and transporting water, nutrients, and sugars between the roots and other parts of the plant. The stem comprises nodes and internodes, with leaves and branches emerging from these critical points. Nodes are essential for forming branches, leaves, and flowers, while internodes determine the spacing between nodes, influencing the plant's overall height.

Leaves are a prominent feature of the cannabis plant and play a vital role in its lifecycle. Typically characterized by a palate or digitate structure, cannabis leaves consist of serrated edges and distinct veins. The leaves serve as the primary site for photosynthesis, the process through which the plant converts light into energy. Trichomes, tiny hair-like structures on the leaves and other plant surfaces, produce cannabinoids, terpenes, and other compounds responsible for the plant's therapeutic and psychoactive effects.

Flowers, or buds, are perhaps the most celebrated part of the cannabis plant. These reproductive structures develop in response to the plant reaching maturity and the onset of the flowering stage. Female cannabis plants produce cannabinoid-rich resin flowers, while male plants produce pollen. The psychoactive compounds, including THC (tetrahydrocannabinol) and CBD (cannabidiol), are concentrated in the flowers, making them the most sought-after part of the plant for both recreational and medicinal use.

Understanding the sex of a cannabis plant is crucial for cultivators, as only female plants produce the desired flower buds. Female flowers are characterized by small, hair-like structures called pistils, while male flowers make pollen sacs. Cannabis plants can also be hermaphroditic, exhibiting both male and female reproductive organs, leading to self-pollination and reduced flower quality.

The reproduction process is essential for the survival of the cannabis species. Pollination occurs when pollen from the male plant reaches the female flower's stigma. Once fertilized, the female plant shifts its energy towards seed production, diverting resources from cannabinoid and resin production. Cultivators often aim to prevent pollination in female plants, promoting the growth of seedless flowers, commonly known as sinsemilla, which are valued for their potency and quality.

Beyond the basic structures, the cannabis plant's anatomy extends to the cellular level. Trichomes, the resin-producing glands on the plant's surface, are particularly significant. These microscopic structures house the cannabinoids, terpenes, and flavonoids that define the plant's chemical profile. The density and maturity of trichomes directly influence the potency and therapeutic properties of the harvested flowers.

Additionally, cannabis plants possess a network of vascular tissues, including the xylem and phloem, for transporting water, nutrients, and sugars. The xylem facilitates the upward movement of water and minerals from the roots to the rest of the plant. At the same time, the phloem transports sugars produced during photosynthesis to various parts of the plant.

Environmental factors play a crucial role in shaping the anatomy of the cannabis plant. The concept of phenotype refers to the observable characteristics of a plant resulting from the interaction between its genetic makeup (genotype) and the environment. Factors such as light intensity, temperature, humidity, and nutrient availability influence the development and expression of specific traits, contributing to the unique features of each cannabis strain.

In conclusion, delving into the anatomy of the cannabis plant reveals a symphony of interconnected structures and processes that define its growth, reproduction, and chemical composition. From the hidden complexity of the root system to the celebrated flowers rich in cannabinoids, every part of the cannabis plant serves a purpose in its lifecycle. Whether approached from a scientific, horticultural, or recreational perspective, a deeper understanding of cannabis anatomy is fundamental for cultivators, researchers, and enthusiasts alike. It not only facilitates successful cultivation practices but also fosters a profound appreciation for this ancient herb's remarkable and versatile nature.

Different Cannabis Strains

The world of cannabis is rich and diverse, boasting a plethora of different strains that cater to a wide array of preferences and medicinal needs. Cannabis strains are essentially variations or subspecies of the Cannabis sativa, Cannabis indica, and Cannabis ruderalis plants, resulting from centuries of cultivation and selective breeding. Each strain has its unique combination of cannabinoids, terpenes, and flavonoids, giving rise to distinct aromas, flavors, and effects. Understanding the characteristics of different cannabis strains is essential for both recreational users seeking specific experiences and medical patients aiming to address particular symptoms.

Cannabis sativa strains are known for their uplifting and energizing effects, making them popular choices for daytime use. Sativa plants typically have tall and narrow structures with long, thin leaves. The high associated with sativa strains is often described as cerebral, providing a sense of creativity, focus, and motivation. Sativas are commonly associated with strains originating from regions near the equator, where the plant has adapted to the longer daylight hours.

On the other end of the spectrum are Cannabis indica strains, renowned for their relaxing and soothing effects. Indica plants are shorter and bushier, with broader leaves than sativa. The high from Indica strains are often more physical, leading to a body-centric experience that can benefit relaxation, pain relief, and sleep. Indica strains are historically associated with regions at higher latitudes, where shorter daylight hours and cooler temperatures prevail.

As the name suggests, hybrid strains result from crossbreeding sativa and indica plants. Combining the desirable traits of both subspecies, hybrid strains offer diverse effects, aromas, and flavors. Hybridization allows cultivators to tailor the characteristics of a strain to meet specific user preferences or medicinal requirements. For example, a sativa-dominant hybrid might provide an uplifting experience with a touch of relaxation. In contrast, an Indica-dominant hybrid could offer a more calming effect with a hint of mental stimulation.

In recent years, the cannabis market has witnessed the emergence of auto-flowering strains, predominantly derived from Cannabis ruderalis genetics. Unlike traditional cannabis strains that rely on changes in light cycles to initiate flowering, auto-flowering plants automatically transition from the vegetative stage to the flowering stage based on age. This unique trait makes them well-suited for outdoor cultivation in regions with unpredictable climates and shorter growing seasons.

Beyond the broad classifications of sativa, indica, hybrid, and auto-flowering, the world of cannabis strains is further diversified by the multitude of cultivars or varieties available. Each cultivar is a distinct genetic expression, often developed through selective breeding to emphasize specific traits. These traits can include the plant's physical characteristics and its cannabinoid and terpene profiles, which play a significant role in the overall experience.

Cannabis strains can be broadly categorized based on their cannabinoid content. For instance, high-THC strains are cultivated for their potent psychoactive effects and are popular among recreational users seeking an intense and euphoric experience. Conversely, high-CBD strains are favored for their non-intoxicating properties and potential therapeutic benefits. CBD (cannabidiol) is a cannabinoid known for its anti-inflammatory, analgesic, and anxiolytic properties, making it a valuable option for medical users seeking relief without the psychoactive effects associated with THC (tetrahydrocannabinol).

Terpenes, aromatic compounds found in cannabis and other plants, contribute significantly to the distinct flavors and aromas of different strains. Terpenes also interact with cannabinoids, influencing the overall effects of a strain through what is known as the entourage effect. For instance, terpene myrcene is associated with sedative effects, while limonene may contribute to an uplifting and mood-enhancing experience. As a result, cannabis enthusiasts and medical users alike often consider the terpene profile of a strain when selecting products. Geographical origin is another factor that influences the characteristics of cannabis strains. Strains originating from specific regions often develop unique traits due to variations in climate, soil composition, and cultivation practices. For example, Hindu Kush mountain range strains, such as Afghan Kush, are renowned for their potent indica effects and earthy flavors. Similarly, strains from the tropical climates of Southeast Asia, like Thai Sativa, may exhibit energetic and uplifting qualities.

In the modern cannabis market, the availability of strains is vast, and new cultivars continue to emerge through innovative breeding techniques. Cannabis enthusiasts can explore a kaleidoscope of flavors, aromas, and effects, ranging from fruity and sweet to earthy and spicy. Some strains are designed for specific purposes, such as enhancing creativity, alleviating pain, or promoting relaxation, allowing users to tailor their cannabis experience to their individual preferences and needs.

Medical cannabis patients often benefit from strains that address specific symptoms or conditions. For instance, strains with high CBD content and a balanced ratio of THC to CBD are commonly used to manage chronic pain, inflammation, anxiety, and epilepsy. Patients seeking relief from insomnia may gravitate towards indica strains with higher levels of myrcene and terpinolene. Meanwhile, those dealing with fatigue or mood disorders may find sativa strains with uplifting terpenes like pinene and limonene more suitable.

As the cannabis industry continues to evolve, the importance of standardized testing and labeling becomes increasingly apparent. Testing facilities analyze cannabis products to determine their cannabinoid and terpene profiles, ensuring accurate labeling and providing consumers with essential information to make informed choices. This transparency is crucial for both recreational users and medical patients, allowing them to select strains that align with their preferences and therapeutic goals.

In conclusion, the world of cannabis strains is a dynamic and ever-expanding landscape, offering a diverse array of choices for enthusiasts and patients alike. From the energizing effects of sativa strains to the relaxing properties of indica varieties and the nuanced experiences provided by hybrid and auto-flowering strains, the cannabis plant continues to captivate and serve the diverse needs of its consumers. As science and cultivation practices advance, the exploration of new strains and the refinement of existing ones will undoubtedly contribute to the ongoing evolution of the cannabis culture, providing an exciting journey for those who seek to discover the endless possibilities within this remarkable plant.

Choosing the Right Strain for Your Needs

Choosing the right cannabis strain is a nuanced and individualized process that involves consideration of various factors to meet specific needs and preferences. The diverse array of strains available in the cannabis market, each with its unique combination of cannabinoids, terpenes, and effects, presents both recreational users and medical patients with an extensive menu of options. The key to a satisfying cannabis experience lies in understanding personal goals, desired effects, and any potential therapeutic benefits sought.

For those exploring cannabis for recreational purposes, the choice of strain often hinges on the desired effects and the overall experience one hopes to achieve. Sativa-dominant strains, with their reputation for uplifting and energizing effects, are popular among individuals seeking a boost in creativity, focus, or sociability. These strains are often chosen for daytime use, as they are less likely to induce sedation or relaxation. Conversely, Indica-dominant strains, known for their relaxing and calming effects, are preferred by those looking to unwind, alleviate stress, or promote sleep. Hybrid strains offer a middle ground, combining sativa and Indica characteristics, providing users with a balanced experience that can be tailored to specific preferences.

Beyond the broad categorization of sativa, indica, and hybrid, the specific cannabinoid content of a strain plays a crucial role in determining its effects. Tetrahydrocannabinol (THC) is the primary psychoactive compound in cannabis, responsible for the euphoric "high" commonly associated with the plant. Strains with higher THC content are chosen by recreational users seeking a more potent and intense experience. On the other hand, cannabidiol (CBD), another prominent cannabinoid, is non-intoxicating and is often selected by those who wish to avoid the psychoactive effects of THC.

High-CBD strains are sought for their potential therapeutic benefits, including anti-inflammatory, analgesic, and anxiolytic properties.

Terpenes, aromatic compounds found in cannabis and various other plants, contribute to the distinct flavors and aromas of different strains and also play a significant role in the overall effects through the entourage effect. For instance, terpene myrcene is associated with sedative effects, while limonene may contribute to an uplifting and mood-enhancing experience. Understanding a strain's terpene profile can help users choose products that align with their sensory preferences and desired effects.

Geographical origin is another consideration when selecting a cannabis strain. Strains originating from specific regions often develop unique traits due to variations in climate, soil composition, and cultivation practices. For example, Hindu Kush Mountain range strains, such as Afghan Kush, are renowned for their potent indica effects and earthy flavors. Similarly, strains from the tropical climates of Southeast Asia, like Thai Sativa, may exhibit energetic and uplifting qualities.

Recreational users may also consider the THC-to-CBD ratio of a strain, as this can influence the balance of psychoactive and therapeutic effects. Strains with a higher THC-to-CBD ratio are likely to produce more pronounced psychoactive effects. In comparison, those with a balanced or higher CBD-to-THC ratio may offer a milder, more therapeutic experience. This consideration becomes especially relevant for users who are sensitive to the psychoactive effects of THC or are seeking a more functional and clear-headed experience.

For medical cannabis patients, the selection of the correct strain often involves addressing specific symptoms or conditions. The therapeutic potential of cannabis lies not only in its ability to induce psychoactive effects but also in its capacity to alleviate various ailments. Patients seeking relief from chronic pain, inflammation, or neuropathy may benefit from strains with a balanced ratio of THC to CBD. CBD's anti-inflammatory and analgesic properties can complement the pain-relieving effects of THC without inducing a robust psychoactive high.

Patients dealing with anxiety or mood disorders may explore strains with higher levels of CBD or specific terpenes known for their anxiolytic properties, such as linalool or beta-caryophyllene. Conversely, those seeking assistance with sleep disorders or insomnia may gravitate towards indica strains with higher levels of myrcene, a terpene associated with sedative effects. The individual response to cannabis can vary, so patients often engage in a process of trial and error to find the strain and dosage that best addresses their specific needs.

In the realm of medical cannabis, patients must communicate openly with healthcare professionals to ensure a tailored and effective treatment plan. Healthcare providers can guide strain selection, dosage, and administration methods based on the patient's medical history, symptoms, and treatment goals. Moreover, medical cannabis patients may have access to products specifically formulated to address specific conditions, with standardized cannabinoid and terpene profiles for consistency and reliability.

Choosing the right strain extends beyond considerations of effects and therapeutic benefits. Practical aspects such as the method of consumption, dosage, and the user's tolerance level also influence the decision-making process. Different consumption methods, such as smoking, vaporizing, edibles, or tinctures, can result in varied onset times and durations of effects. Novice users may opt for strains with lower THC content to mitigate the risk of overwhelming psychoactive effects, gradually increasing the dosage as tolerance develops.

Furthermore, the importance of understanding the legality and regulations surrounding cannabis use cannot be overstated. In regions where cannabis is legal, users have the opportunity to access a broader range of strains and products. However, in areas where cannabis remains prohibited or restricted, users may face limitations in strain availability. They may need to explore alternative methods of access, such as medical cannabis programs or CBD products derived from industrial hemp.

Environmental factors also play a role in the cultivation and availability of specific strains. Some strains thrive in particular climates, and the cultivation environment can impact the expression of cannabinoids and terpenes. Users interested in strains with unique regional characteristics may find that locally sourced products better capture the essence of those specific strains. Cultivators and dispensaries often provide information about their products' cultivation practices and genetics, aiding users in making informed choices.

In conclusion, choosing the right cannabis strain is a multifaceted decision that requires thoughtful consideration of individual preferences, desired effects, and potential therapeutic benefits. Whether for recreational enjoyment or medicinal purposes, users can navigate the diverse world of cannabis strains by understanding the interplay between cannabinoids, terpenes, and personal factors such as tolerance and preferred consumption methods. Seeking guidance from healthcare professionals, budtenders, or experienced users and staying informed about local regulations and strain characteristics contribute to a more informed and satisfying cannabis experience. As the cannabis landscape continues to evolve, the exploration of new strains and the refinement of existing ones offer a continuous journey of discovery and customization for enthusiasts and patients alike.

CHAPTER II

Setting Up Your Cannabis Growing Space

Indoor vs. Outdoor Cultivation

The choice between indoor and outdoor cultivation is a pivotal decision for cannabis cultivators, each method offering distinct advantages and challenges. Indoor cultivation provides growers with a controlled environment, precisely regulating temperature, humidity, and light cycles. This level of control facilitates year-round cultivation, making it an attractive option for those seeking a consistent and predictable harvest schedule. Indoor setups typically involve artificial lighting, ventilation systems, and other technologies to recreate optimal growing conditions. This approach enables cultivators to select from a wide range of cannabis strains, regardless of their native climate, and to experiment with various cultivation techniques.

One of the primary advantages of indoor cultivation is the ability to achieve higher yields and potency. By manipulating environmental variables, growers can create conditions that maximize plant growth and cannabinoid production. This level of precision allows for implementing advanced training techniques, such as low-stress training (LST) or screen of green (SCROG), to optimize light penetration and canopy distribution. Additionally, indoor cultivation minimizes the risk of pests and diseases, as the enclosed space provides a barrier against external threats. This control over the growing environment translates into a consistent and potentially higher-quality product, making it particularly appealing to commercial cultivators and those seeking a premium cannabis experience.

However, the advantages of indoor cultivation come with associated costs, both in terms of financial investment and energy consumption. Setting up and maintaining an indoor grow operation requires a significant upfront investment in equipment, such as grow lights, ventilation systems, air conditioning, and environmental controls. The ongoing operational costs, including electricity for lighting and climate control, can be substantial. Moreover, the environmental impact of indoor cultivation, particularly in regions where electricity is generated from non-renewable sources, raises concerns about sustainability. Despite these challenges, advancements in energy-efficient technologies and a growing emphasis on sustainability in the cannabis industry aim to mitigate the environmental footprint of indoor cultivation.

On the other hand, outdoor cultivation leverages the power of natural sunlight and the earth's ecosystem to nurture cannabis plants. Cultivating cannabis outdoors allows growers to harness the sun's full spectrum, providing an honest and cost-effective light source. The expansive outdoor setting enables the cultivation of larger plant populations, making it a suitable choice for those who prioritize quantity over the precision of control. Outdoor cultivation is often favored by small-scale or hobbyist growers who may need more resources for an indoor setup.

One of the significant advantages of outdoor cultivation is the reduced operational cost compared to indoor methods. Natural sunlight eliminates the need for expensive artificial lighting, and the open environment minimizes elaborate ventilation systems. This cost-effectiveness is especially appealing for cultivators in regions with abundant sunlight and favorable climates. Outdoor cultivation also capitalizes on the symbiotic relationship between plants and their natural surroundings, fostering a more sustainable and ecologically balanced approach to cannabis cultivation.

While outdoor cultivation offers economic and environmental benefits, it has. The reliance on natural conditions makes outdoor cultivation highly dependent on seasonal changes, with harvests typically occurring in the fall. This limitation may not align with the year-round demand for cannabis in some markets. Furthermore, outdoor cultivation is susceptible to weather variations, pests, and diseases impacting plant health and yield. Cultivators often employ organic pest control methods, companion planting, and strategic crop rotation to address these challenges and promote a healthy and resilient growing environment.

Regulatory considerations also influence the choice between indoor and outdoor cultivation. In regions with legalized or regulated cannabis markets, authorities may impose restrictions on cultivation methods, requiring adherence to specific guidelines regarding security, environmental impact, and product testing. Compliance with these regulations can influence a cultivator's decision to pursue indoor or outdoor cultivation.

In recent years, greenhouse cultivation has gained popularity as a hybrid approach combining elements of both indoor and outdoor methods. Greenhouses provide a controlled environment similar to indoor cultivation but utilize natural sunlight, reducing energy costs compared to fully indoor setups. Greenhouses offer the advantage of extended growing seasons, allowing cultivators to bridge the gap between indoor and outdoor cultivation. This flexibility has positioned greenhouse cultivation as a middle-ground option that balances control and sustainability.

Ultimately, the decision between indoor and outdoor cultivation hinges on the cultivator's goals, resources, and preferences. Indoor cultivation appeals to those who prioritize control, consistency, and the ability to cultivate specific strains regardless of external conditions. The controlled environment enables the implementation of advanced techniques and technologies to optimize plant growth and maximize yield. In contrast, outdoor cultivation resonates with cultivators who value sustainability, reduced operational costs, and a more natural approach to cannabis cultivation. The open environment of outdoor cultivation connects the plant to its ecological context, contributing to a unique terroir that can influence the final product.

In conclusion, the choice between indoor and outdoor cultivation is a multifaceted decision that involves weighing the advantages and challenges of each method. Whether driven by the desire for precise control, sustainability, or a combination of both, cultivators navigate these considerations to align their cultivation practices with their goals and values. As the cannabis industry continues to evolve, advancements in technology, sustainability practices, and regulatory frameworks will shape the landscape of cultivation methods, providing cultivators with a spectrum of options to meet the demands of a dynamic and growing market.

Essential Tools and Equipment

Cultivating cannabis successfully, whether indoors or outdoors, requires the use of essential tools and equipment to create an optimal environment for plant growth. These tools are instrumental in ensuring that cultivators can monitor and control various factors that influence the health, development, and overall yield of cannabis plants. For indoor cultivation, lighting is a cornerstone tool. High-quality grow lights, such as LEDs or high-pressure sodium (HPS) lamps, provide the necessary light spectrum for photosynthesis during the vegetative and flowering stages. Materials like mylar or reflective paint are often used to maximize light distribution and prevent energy waste. Ventilation systems with exhaust fans and intake vents are essential to maintain a controlled environment. These systems regulate temperature, humidity, and CO_2 levels, which are crucial for healthy plant development.

Temperature and humidity control are pivotal for successful cultivation, and to achieve this, growers employ environmental control tools. Air conditioning units and dehumidifiers help maintain optimal temperature and humidity levels, preventing issues like mold and mildew that can compromise the crop. In more extensive operations, automated climate control systems, equipped with sensors and controllers, automatically monitor and adjust environmental parameters. In addition to environmental control, nutrient delivery systems play a crucial role. Hydroponic systems, such as nutrient film technique (NFT) or deep water culture (DWC), allow direct nutrient delivery to the plant roots, maximizing nutrient uptake and promoting vigorous growth.

For outdoor cultivation, the primary consideration is the quality of the soil. Cultivators often use soil testing kits to assess nutrient levels, pH, and other soil characteristics. This information guides the addition of fertilizers and amendments to optimize the soil for cannabis cultivation. To ensure proper irrigation, hoses, drip systems, or soaker hoses are commonly used, enabling cultivators to provide consistent water to their plants. Protective measures are also crucial for outdoor cultivation. Netting or trellises may be employed to support the weight of large cannabis plants and prevent branches from breaking under the load of developing buds.

Another essential tool for both indoor and outdoor cultivation is a reliable pH meter. Monitoring and adjusting the pH of the growing medium is critical for nutrient absorption, as cannabis plants thrive in a specific pH range. pH meters help cultivators maintain this balance, preventing nutrient deficiencies or toxicities impacting plant health. In addition to pH meters, electrical conductivity (EC) meters are employed to measure nutrient concentrations in the growing medium, ensuring the plants receive the appropriate levels of essential elements.

Propagation tools are indispensable for growers aiming to produce their clones or seeds. Propagation domes, cloning gel or powder, and heat mats aid in creating a conducive environment for the development of healthy roots. In addition, pH-balanced water or a cloning solution is crucial for preventing stress and promoting successful cloning. For those who prefer cultivating from seeds, germination trays and seedling heat mats can enhance germination, providing an optimal environment for seedling development.

The importance of pruning and trimming tools cannot be overstated in cannabis cultivation. Pruning shears, trimming scissors, and loppers are essential for maintaining plant health, shaping the canopy, and removing unwanted growth. These tools are particularly vital during the flowering stage when cultivators may need to selectively trim leaves or branches to improve light penetration and airflow, enhancing bud development and preventing mold issues.

Environmental monitoring tools, such as hygrometers, temperature gauges, and CO2 meters, offer cultivators insights into the growing environment. Regular monitoring allows for timely adjustments to environmental conditions, optimizing plant growth. Advanced cultivation setups often incorporate data loggers or smart controllers that automate the monitoring and adjustment processes, providing real-time data and control capabilities through digital interfaces.

Pest control tools are crucial for preventing and managing infestations that can threaten the health of cannabis plants. Insect nets, sticky traps, and predatory insects are commonly used as preventive measures. Organic pesticides and insecticidal soaps are employed to address pest issues without compromising the quality and safety of the final product. Regular scouting and early intervention are critical components of an effective pest management strategy.

Cultivators rely on harvesting and drying tools to ensure a successful and high-quality harvest. Sharp, clean pruning shears or scissors are used for precise harvesting, minimizing plant damage. Drying racks, screens, and dehumidifiers are essential for the drying process, preventing mold and preserving the flavor and potency of the harvested buds. Once dried, storage containers such as glass jars with humidity packs cure and store the final product, enhancing its overall quality.

In soil cultivation, tillers, shovels, and rakes are foundational for preparing outdoor grow spaces. These tools aid in breaking up soil, removing debris, and creating an optimal planting environment. Mulching tools, like wood chips or straw, are often used to retain moisture, suppress weeds, and insulate the soil. Additionally, compost bins or tumblers support sustainable cultivation practices by allowing cultivators to recycle organic waste into nutrient-rich compost, contributing to healthy soil structure and fertility.

As the cannabis industry evolves, innovative technologies and tools continue to emerge. For example, light-emitting diode (LED) grow lights are gaining popularity in indoor cultivation due to their energy efficiency and customizable light spectrums. Automated irrigation systems equipped with timers and sensors provide precise control over watering schedules. Intelligent controllers and monitoring devices connected to the Internet of Things (IoT) enable remote monitoring and control, allowing cultivators to manage their operations from afar. These advancements enhance efficiency, reduce labor requirements, and contribute to the overall success of cannabis cultivation endeavors.

In conclusion, essential tools and equipment form the backbone of successful cannabis cultivation, providing cultivators with the means to create and maintain optimal growing conditions. Whether cultivated indoors or outdoors, these tools contribute to environmental control, nutrient management, propagation, pest control, and harvesting processes. Each tool is vital in maximizing yield, potency, and overall crop quality, from traditional tools like pruning shears and pH meters to innovative technologies such as intelligent controllers and LED grow lights. As the cannabis industry grows, cultivators will benefit from staying abreast of technological advancements and incorporating tools that align with their cultivation goals and sustainability practices.

Creating an Optimal Growing Environment

Creating an optimal growing environment is a fundamental aspect of successful cannabis cultivation, whether the cultivation is conducted indoors or outdoors. The cultivation environment directly influences the health, development, and overall yield of cannabis plants, making it crucial for growers to carefully consider and manipulate various factors to provide an ideal setting for plant growth. In indoor cultivation, achieving this optimal environment begins with controlling light conditions. High-quality grow lights, such as LEDs or high-pressure sodium (HPS) lamps, provide the necessary light spectrum for photosynthesis during the vegetative and flowering stages. Light cycles are carefully regulated to mimic natural daylight and darkness, with different cycles used for the vegetative and flowering stages to optimize plant growth.

Alongside lighting, maintaining an appropriate temperature is paramount. Cannabis plants thrive within a specific temperature range, generally between 70-85°F (21-29°C) during the day and slightly more incredible at night. Air conditioning and ventilation systems with exhaust fans and intake vents are crucial for managing temperature levels. These systems help maintain optimal temperatures and ensure proper air circulation, preventing the buildup of heat and humidity that can lead to issues such as mold and mildew.

Humidity control is another critical aspect of creating an optimal indoor growing environment. Cannabis plants have varying humidity needs during different stages of growth. For instance, higher humidity is generally required during the vegetative stage, while lower humidity levels are favored during the flowering stage. Dehumidifiers are commonly used to reduce excess humidity, especially in tightly sealed indoor environments where moisture can accumulate. Striking the right balance in humidity levels contributes to healthy plant development and prevents the onset of environmental stressors.

In addition to temperature and humidity, carbon dioxide (CO2) levels are crucial in optimizing plant growth. Cannabis plants use CO2 during photosynthesis to convert light into energy. While outdoor cultivation naturally benefits from atmospheric CO2, indoor environments may require supplementation. CO2 generators or tanks enhance CO2 levels, particularly in well-sealed indoor grow spaces. Careful monitoring and adjustment of CO2 levels contribute to increased photosynthetic activity, promoting robust plant growth and higher yields.

Nutrient delivery systems are integral to indoor cultivation setups. Hydroponic systems, such as nutrient film technique (NFT) or deep-water culture (DWC), allow for precise nutrient delivery directly to the plant roots. This approach maximizes nutrient uptake and promotes vigorous growth. Soil-based cultivation, on the other hand, relies on the use of high-quality potting mixes and organic or synthetic fertilizers to provide essential nutrients. Maintaining the correct nutrient balance is critical for preventing deficiencies or toxicities that adversely affect plant health.

While indoor cultivation provides a controlled environment, outdoor cultivation leverages natural sunlight and environmental elements; creating an optimal outdoor growing environment begins with selecting an appropriate site. Factors such as sunlight exposure, soil quality, and water availability are considered when choosing the outdoor cultivation location. The cultivation site should receive ample sunlight throughout the day, ensuring cannabis plants receive the necessary light for photosynthesis.

Soil preparation is a crucial step in outdoor cultivation. Testing the soil's nutrient content, pH levels, and structure helps determine the amendments required to create a nutrient-rich, well-draining growing medium. Cultivators often incorporate organic matter, compost, and other soil amendments to enhance soil fertility. Mulching tools like wood chips or straws may retain moisture, suppress weeds, and regulate soil temperature, contributing to a healthy and balanced outdoor growing environment.

Irrigation is another essential component of outdoor cultivation. Hoses, drip systems, or soaker hoses are commonly used to provide consistent and adequate water to cannabis plants. Proper irrigation practices prevent drought stress, support healthy plant development, and contribute to optimal yields. Depending on the local climate and water availability, some outdoor cultivators may install rainwater collection systems or utilize sustainable irrigation practices to minimize environmental impact.

Environmental monitoring is crucial in indoor and outdoor cultivation to ensure conditions remain within the desired range. Hygrometers, temperature gauges, and CO_2 meters provide real-time data on the growing environment for indoor cultivation. Automated climate control systems equipped with sensors and controllers offer precision in maintaining optimal conditions. Cultivators regularly monitor weather patterns, soil moisture levels, and overall plant health in outdoor cultivation to identify issues and make timely adjustments.

Protection against pests and diseases is a universal concern for cannabis cultivators. In indoor environments, the controlled setting minimizes the risk of pest infestations, but vigilance and preventive measures remain essential. Integrated pest management (IPM) strategies, including using beneficial insects, organic pesticides, and regular monitoring, help prevent and address pest issues without harmful chemicals. Outdoor cultivation, with its exposure to natural elements, presents a greater risk of pest and disease challenges. Cultivators often employ preventive measures, such as companion planting, natural predators, and organic pesticides, to maintain a healthy and resilient outdoor growing environment.

The choice of cannabis strains also contributes to the creation of an optimal growing environment. Selecting well-suited strains to the local climate and environmental conditions is crucial for maximizing yield and potency. Strains adapted to the specific region's temperature, sunlight, and humidity levels are more likely to thrive and produce high-quality buds. Understanding the phenotypic expression of strains and their adaptability to local conditions enables cultivators to make informed decisions that align with the unique characteristics of their cultivation environment.

Creating an optimal growing environment is an ongoing process that requires constant monitoring and adjustment. Cultivators must be responsive to changes in the weather, seasonal variations, and the evolving needs of the plants. Regular observation of plant health, nutrient requirements, and environmental conditions allows for proactive interventions, minimizing the risk of issues that could impact the final yield. Whether cultivated indoors or outdoors, the commitment to creating an optimal growing environment is a foundational practice that sets the stage for successful and sustainable cannabis cultivation.

CHAPTER III

Germination and Seedling Care

Germination Techniques

Germination is a critical stage in cannabis cultivation, marking the beginning of a plant's life cycle. Successful germination lays the foundation for healthy seedlings, robust vegetative growth, and a bountiful harvest. Cultivators employ various techniques to initiate and optimize the germination process, whether starting from seeds or clones.

When germinating cannabis seeds, growers often choose between different methods, each with its advantages and considerations. One common technique is the paper towel method. In this approach, cannabis seeds are placed between moist paper towels, creating a humid environment conducive to germination. The paper towels are then sealed in a plastic bag, maintaining moisture levels. This method is famous for its simplicity and accessibility, requiring minimal equipment. However, care must be taken to prevent the paper towels from drying out or becoming too wet, as both extremes can impede germination.

Another popular germination technique involves planting seeds directly in a growing medium, such as soil or a soilless mix. Cultivators create a small hole in the medium, place the seed at a suitable depth, and cover it with a layer of soil. Adequate moisture is essential to ensure that the growing medium remains consistently damp, providing the ideal conditions for germination. This method is straightforward and eliminates the need for transplanting seedlings, reducing potential stress on the delicate plants.

Germination cubes or plugs are also widely used in cannabis cultivation. These small, pre-formed containers are designed to provide an optimal environment for germination. Cannabis seeds are placed directly into the cubes and kept moist to encourage germination. Germination cubes are advantageous for their convenience and ability to support seedlings' early growth. Once the seedlings have developed roots and a few sets of leaves, they can be transplanted into larger containers or directly into the final growing medium.

Hydroponic systems offer an alternative germination method, particularly for cultivators utilizing hydroponic or aeroponic setups. In these systems, cannabis seeds are placed in a specialized propagator or floating device, allowing the emerging seedlings access to nutrient-rich water. Hydroponic germination provides a controlled environment with precise control over nutrient levels and pH. This method is favored for its efficiency and suitability for hydroponic cultivation.

For those who prefer a hands-off approach to germination, germination trays, and seedling heat mats offer a set-it-and-forget-it solution. Seeds are placed directly into pre-formed cells or compartments in the germination tray, and the entire tray is set on a seedling heat mat. The heat mat provides a consistent and gentle warmth, creating optimal conditions for germination. This method is prevalent for its simplicity and the ability to germinate multiple seeds simultaneously.

Regardless of the germination technique chosen, maintaining an appropriate temperature is crucial for success. Cannabis seeds generally require temperatures between 70-85°F (21-29°C) for optimal germination. Seedling heat mats or a warm and consistently heated environment help ensure the seeds receive the necessary warmth to trigger germination.

Light exposure during germination is another consideration. While cannabis seeds do not require light to germinate, providing a low-intensity light source, such as fluorescent or LED lights, can be beneficial. This minimal light exposure helps guide emerging seedlings upward and encourages healthy growth. Once the seedlings have developed their first set of true leaves, they can be transitioned to more intense light conditions suitable for the vegetative stage.

Cloning, an alternative to seed germination, involves taking cuttings from a mature cannabis plant and encouraging them to develop into independent, genetically identical plants. The cloning process typically begins with selecting a healthy and well-established "mother" plant with desirable characteristics. A cutting, or clone, is taken from the mother plant, typically from a growing tip with several nodes. The cutting is then treated with rooting hormones to encourage root development and placed in a growing medium, such as rock wool cubes or a soilless mix.

Maintaining high humidity is crucial for successful cloning, as it helps prevent excessive moisture loss through the leaves before the roots have developed. Humidity domes or propagators are commonly used to create a humid microenvironment around the clones. Additionally, providing a consistent temperature between 70-75°F (21-24°C) promotes optimal rooting.

Aeroponic cloning systems represent an advanced technique for cultivating clones. Clones are suspended in a chamber in these systems, and nutrient-rich mist is continuously sprayed onto the stems. This method accelerates root development, as the suspended clones have increased access to oxygen and nutrients. Aeroponic cloning is valued for its efficiency and high success rates but requires careful monitoring and maintenance.

Ensuring a sterile and contamination-free environment is crucial regardless of the germination or cloning technique chosen. Contaminants, such as mold or bacteria, can compromise the health of seeds or clones, leading to poor germination rates or weak plants. Using clean, sterilized equipment and providing proper ventilation and air circulation helps minimize the risk of contamination during the early stages of plant development.

Once germination or cloning is successful, the next phase involves transitioning seedlings or clones to the vegetative stage. This stage is characterized by vigorous growth, the development of multiple leaves, and the establishment of a robust root system. Cultivators often transplant seedlings or clones into larger containers with nutrient-rich soil or growing medium to support their continued growth.

During the vegetative stage, providing appropriate light is crucial. Cannabis plants thrive under a light cycle of 18 hours followed by 6 hours of darkness. High-intensity discharge (HID) lights, LEDs, or other suitable grow lights provide the necessary light spectrum for robust vegetative growth. As the plants develop, cultivators may employ training techniques, such as topping or low-stress training (LST), to promote bushier growth and enhance light penetration.

Nutrient requirements during the vegetative stage differ from those during germination or cloning. While cannabis seeds or clones initially rely on the nutrients stored within them, vegetative-stage plants benefit from additional nutrients to support their rapid growth. Balanced fertilizers containing nitrogen, phosphorus, potassium, and secondary and micronutrients are commonly used during this stage. Cultivators adjust nutrient concentrations based on the specific needs of their plants, monitoring for any signs of nutrient deficiencies or excesses.

Environmental conditions, including temperature and humidity, remain essential during vegetative. Cannabis plants generally thrive in temperatures between 70-85°F (21-29°C) with humidity levels ranging from 40-60%. Adequate ventilation and air circulation help prevent issues such as mold or mildew. Proper spacing between plants ensures that each plant receives sufficient light and airflow.

After a suitable period of vegetative growth, cultivators transition their plants to the flowering stage by adjusting the light cycle to 12 hours of light followed by 12 hours of darkness. This change in light triggers the plants to shift their focus from vegetative growth to the development of flowers or buds. The flowering stage is characterized by the emergence of pistils, the development of resinous trichomes, and the production of cannabinoids and terpenes.

Throughout the flowering stage, cultivators continue to monitor and adjust environmental conditions to optimize bud development. Temperature control becomes increasingly critical, as fluctuations can impact the formation of cannabinoids and terpenes. Maintaining temperatures between 65-80°F (18-27°C) helps promote the production of desirable compounds while preventing heat-related stress.

Humidity levels are carefully managed to minimize the risk of mold or bud rot, which can be more prevalent in the dense buds of the flowering stage. Cultivators gradually reduce humidity levels during this stage, aiming for a 40-50% range. Adequate airflow and ventilation help maintain optimal humidity levels and prevent stagnant air pockets within the canopy.

Nutrient requirements shift during the flowering stage, emphasizing phosphorus and potassium more. Phosphorus promotes flower development and enhances bud structure, while potassium contributes to plant health and resilience. Cultivators may transition to bloom- specific fertilizers or adjust nutrient ratios to meet the changing needs of flowering plants. Monitoring nutrient levels and adjusting formulations based on plant response are critical practices during this crucial stage.

Advanced cultivation techniques, such as defoliation or lollipopping, may be employed during the flowering stage to enhance light penetration and promote even bud development. These techniques involve selectively removing leaves or lower branches to redirect energy toward developing top colas. However, cultivators must exercise caution to avoid excessive stress on the plants, as this can negatively impact yield and quality.

The final weeks of the flowering stage are marked by the maturation of the buds and the accumulation of cannabinoids and terpenes. As the trichomes transition from clear to cloudy or amber, cultivators determine the optimal harvest time based on the final product's desired effects and characteristics. Harvesting involves carefully trimming the buds, removing excess leaves, and preparing the crop for drying and curing.

Drying and curing are essential steps in the post-harvest process that significantly impact the quality and potency of the final product. Drying involves hanging trimmed buds in a controlled environment with proper ventilation. This process allows for gradually removing moisture from the buds while preserving cannabinoids and terpenes. After drying, the buds are cured in sealed containers, such as glass jars, for several weeks. Curing enhances the final product's flavor, aroma, and smoothness by promoting the breakdown of chlorophyll and facilitating the development of complex terpene profiles.

In conclusion, germination techniques are the initial steps in the cannabis cultivation journey, setting the stage for a successful and productive growing cycle. Whether germinating seeds or cultivating clones, cultivators choose methods that align with their preferences, equipment, and cultivation goals. Successful germination leads to healthy seedlings or clones, which, when provided with optimal conditions during the vegetative and flowering stages, can result in a bountiful harvest of high-quality cannabis. The cultivation process is a dynamic and multifaceted endeavor, requiring knowledge, skill, and attention to detail to navigate the various stages and produce a final product that meets the desired potency, flavor, and aroma standards.

Proper Handling of Seedlings

The proper handling of seedlings is a crucial aspect of cannabis cultivation, influencing the trajectory of the plant's growth and overall health throughout its life cycle. From the moment seeds germinate, or clones take root, cultivators must exercise care and precision in managing the delicate seedlings. The initial stages of a cannabis plant's life are marked by vulnerability, and providing the right conditions and attention is essential for fostering robust and healthy development.

When seedlings emerge from the germination process, whether through the paper towel method, direct planting in a growing medium, or other techniques, they are delicate and sensitive to their environment. The first consideration is transplanting these seedlings into a suitable growing medium. Whether transitioning from a germination cube, plug, or other starting medium, gently transferring the seedlings to their next home requires a delicate touch. Cultivators aim to minimize stress during this process by carefully handling the seedlings and avoiding damage to the fragile roots and stems. Choosing an appropriate growing medium that provides the necessary nutrients and aeration further supports the seedlings' transition to the vegetative stage.

Lighting is critical in adequately handling seedlings, particularly during their early development stages. Seedlings benefit from a consistent and suitable light source that promotes healthy growth. High-intensity discharge (HID) lights, fluorescent lights, or light-emitting diodes (LEDs) with a spectrum optimized for vegetative growth are commonly used. Positioning the lights at the proper distance from the seedlings prevents stretching and ensures they receive an adequate light intensity. As seedlings grow, adjusting the height of the lights to maintain an optimal balance helps prevent issues such as light burn while encouraging sturdy and compact growth.

Proper watering is a fundamental consideration in the care of seedlings. Overwatering or underwatering can pose risks to the delicate balance of the developing plants. Cannabis seedlings prefer a consistently moist but not waterlogged growing medium. Providing water with a pH level within the optimal range ensures that nutrient uptake is not compromised. Small, controlled watering sessions, rather than heavy drenching, prevent the risk of waterlogged soil and promote the development of a healthy root system. As the seedlings mature, adjusting watering practices according to their needs and growth stages becomes crucial.

Nutrient management is another facet of handling seedlings with precision. While the initial stages of seedling development may not require additional nutrients beyond those in the growing medium, monitoring for signs of nutrient deficiencies or excesses is essential. As seedlings progress to the vegetative stage, adjusting nutrient formulations to their changing requirements supports vigorous growth. Carefully observing the plants for any indications of nutrient-related issues, such as yellowing leaves or stunted growth, allows cultivators to make timely adjustments to their feeding regimen.

Temperature and humidity control contribute significantly to the proper handling of seedlings. Cannabis seedlings thrive in a stable and moderate environment. Maintaining temperatures within the range of 70-85°F (21-29°C) encourages optimal growth while avoiding extremes that could stress the plants. Humidity levels should be adjusted according to the stage of development, with slightly higher humidity favored during the early stages to prevent excessive moisture loss through transpiration. As the seedlings grow, gradually lowering humidity levels helps prepare them to transition to the flowering stage.

Ventilation and airflow are critical components of the growing environment for seedlings. Proper air circulation helps prevent the development of stagnant air pockets, reducing the risk of mold or mildew. Gentle airflow around the seedlings strengthens their stems and promotes sturdy growth. However, care must be taken to avoid direct and excessive airflow that could lead to stress or drying out of the seedlings. Striking the right balance in ventilation ensures a healthy and well-ventilated environment for the developing plants.

Handling seedlings also involves monitoring for potential pests and diseases. While seedlings are generally less susceptible to pests than more mature plants, vigilance is crucial. Integrated pest management (IPM) practices, such as regular inspection, the introduction of beneficial insects, and the use of organic pesticides, help prevent and address pest issues without compromising the health of the seedlings. Maintaining a clean, sterile environment, including sanitized equipment and growing containers, minimizes disease risk.

As seedlings progress through the vegetative stage, they develop a more robust structure, including a well-established root system and multiple sets of leaves. At this stage, handling seedlings may involve training techniques to shape their growth. Low-stress training (LST), topping, or defoliation are methods employed by cultivators to encourage bushier growth, enhance light penetration, and create an even canopy. These techniques are executed with a gentle touch to avoid causing stress or damage to the plants. Observing the seedlings' response to training helps cultivators adjust their approach to achieve the desired growth patterns.

The transition from the vegetative stage to the flowering stage represents a critical juncture in the life of cannabis seedlings. As the plants begin to show signs of sexual maturity, cultivators must discern and manage the sex of the plants, removing any males to prevent pollination and ensure the development of seedless buds. This process requires a keen eye and careful examination of the pre-flowers that indicate the sex of the plants. Proper handling of seedlings during this stage involves promptly identifying and segregating male and female plants.

The final weeks of the flowering stage bring the anticipation of harvest. Proper handling of seedlings at this stage involves monitoring trichome development to determine the optimal time for harvest. Trichomes, the resinous glands that contain cannabinoids and terpenes, transition from clear to cloudy or amber, signaling the peak of cannabinoid production. Harvesting involves careful trimming of the mature buds, removing excess leaves, and preparing the crop for drying and curing.

Drying and curing are essential steps in the post-harvest handling of cannabis plants. After carefully harvesting the mature buds, cultivators hang them in a controlled environment with proper ventilation to remove moisture gradually. Depending on environmental conditions, the drying process typically takes a week or more. Once dried, the buds are cured in sealed containers, such as glass jars, for several weeks. Curing enhances the final product's flavor, aroma, and smoothness by allowing the breakdown of chlorophyll and the development of complex terpene profiles.

In conclusion, the proper handling of seedlings is a nuanced and multifaceted aspect of cannabis cultivation that spans the entire life cycle of the plant. From the delicate emergence of seedlings in the germination stage to the careful training and management during the vegetative and flowering stages, cultivators play a crucial role in shaping the growth and development of their plants. Precision in environmental control, watering, nutrient management, and pest prevention contributes to the overall health and vitality of cannabis seedlings. As cultivators navigate each stage of the plant's life, combining knowledge, experience, and attentive care ensures the successful cultivation of robust and high-quality cannabis plants.

Importance of the Early Growth Stage

The early growth stage of cannabis plants is a pivotal period that lays the foundation for the entire cultivation journey. Beginning with germination and extending into the vegetative stage, this initial phase is marked by developing seedlings into robust young plants. The importance of the early growth stage cannot be overstated, as it sets the trajectory for the overall health, structure, and productivity of cannabis plants.

Germination marks the commencement of the early growth stage, and its significance cannot be understated. During germination, dormant seeds awaken to life, initiating the process of root and shoot development. The successful emergence of seedlings from their protective shells is a testament to the viability of the seeds and the cultivator's adherence to proper germination techniques.

The delicate nature of seedlings during this phase necessitates a controlled and nurturing environment. Factors such as temperature, humidity, light, and moisture must be carefully managed to ensure optimal conditions for germination and early seedling growth.

As the seedlings emerge, cultivators transition to the vegetative stage, a period of robust growth and the development of the plant's structural framework. The importance of the early vegetative stage lies in establishing a solid root system and the growth of healthy leaves and branches. During this phase, the focus is on creating a well-balanced and resilient plant structure that can support the eventual weight of mature buds. Vigorous growth in the early vegetative stage lays the groundwork for a sturdy plant capable of withstanding the challenges of later stages, including the flowering phase.

Lighting plays a pivotal role in the early growth stage, especially in the vegetative phase when plants are actively photosynthesizing to produce energy for growth. Providing the right spectrum, intensity, and duration of light is crucial for promoting healthy leaf development and overall plant vigor. High-intensity discharge (HID) lights, fluorescent lights, or light-emitting diodes (LEDs) with a spectrum optimized for vegetative growth are commonly used. The plant establishes its canopy in the early growth stage, and proper lighting practices help prevent issues such as stretching, ensuring compact and robust growth.

Nutrient management is another critical aspect during the early growth stage. While germinating seeds rely on the nutrients stored within them, transitioning to the vegetative stage requires additional nutritional support. Providing a balanced fertilizer with the right mix of nitrogen, phosphorus, potassium, and essential micronutrients is crucial for promoting healthy growth. Early detection and correction of nutrient deficiencies or excesses are critical during this phase to prevent stunted growth and ensure the development of a vigorous plant structure.

Watering practices are equally important in the early growth stage. While seedlings prefer a consistently moist environment, overwatering or underwatering can harm their delicate root systems. Proper irrigation practices involve maintaining a balance between keeping the growing medium adequately moist and avoiding waterlogged conditions. Adjusting the watering frequency and volume according to their increasing needs as the plants grow supports healthy root development and overall growth.

Temperature and humidity control contribute significantly to the success of the early growth stage. Cannabis plants thrive within a specific temperature range, generally between 70-85°F (21-29°C). Maintaining these temperatures fosters optimal metabolic activity and photosynthesis, promoting vigorous growth. Humidity levels are carefully managed, with slightly higher humidity favored during the early stages to prevent excessive moisture loss through transpiration. As the plants mature, gradually lowering humidity levels helps prepare them to transition to the flowering stage.

Ventilation and airflow are essential to a healthy growing environment in the early growth stage. Proper air circulation prevents the development of stagnant air pockets, reducing the risk of mold or mildew. Gentle airflow around the plants strengthens their stems, promotes sturdy growth, and helps prevent heat stress. Adequate spacing between plants ensures that each receives sufficient light and airflow, contributing to a well-ventilated and disease-resistant environment.

The early growth stage is also a time when cultivators may employ training techniques to shape the growth of their plants. Low-stress training (LST), topping, or pruning may encourage bushier growth, enhance light penetration, and create an even canopy. These techniques are applied gently to avoid causing plant stress or damage. Proper training during early growth contributes to developing a well-structured plant that maximizes light exposure and airflow.

Beyond the physical aspects of growth, the early growth stage is a critical period for monitoring the overall health of the plants. Regular observation allows cultivators to promptly identify and address any issues related to pests, diseases, or environmental stressors. Integrated pest management (IPM) practices, such as using beneficial insects, organic pesticides, and regular inspections, help prevent and mitigate potential challenges. A clean and sterile environment, including sanitized equipment and growing containers, minimizes disease risk during this vulnerable phase.

The significance of the early growth stage extends beyond the vegetative phase and into the flowering stage, influencing the final yield and quality of the harvest. A well-established and healthy plant structure developed during the early growth stage is better equipped to support the weight of mature buds. The foundation regarding root development, canopy structure, and overall plant resilience contributes to the plant's ability to efficiently uptake nutrients and produce cannabinoids and terpenes during the flowering phase.

In conclusion, the importance of the early growth stage in cannabis cultivation cannot be overstated. From germination to establishing a robust vegetative structure, this phase shapes the trajectory of the plant's development and influences its ultimate productivity. Providing optimal conditions, including lighting, nutrient management, watering practices, and environmental control, ensures the healthy growth of seedlings into sturdy and resilient young plants. As cultivators navigate the intricacies of the early growth stage, their attention to detail and proactive care set the stage for a successful cultivation journey, culminating in a bountiful and high-quality harvest.

CHAPTER IV

The Vegetative Stage

Nutrient Requirements

Nutrient requirements are critical to successful cannabis cultivation, influencing the plant's growth, development, and ultimate yield. Understanding the essential nutrients and their role in various stages of the cannabis life cycle is fundamental to providing optimal plant conditions. The primary nutrients required by cannabis plants include nitrogen (N), phosphorus (P), and potassium (K), often referred to as N-P-K, along with secondary nutrients and micronutrients.

During the early growth stages, particularly in the vegetative phase, cannabis plants have a heightened need for nitrogen. Nitrogen is a critical component of chlorophyll, the green pigment responsible for photosynthesis. Adequate nitrogen promotes healthy leaf development, vigorous growth, and the establishment of a robust canopy. In this phase, cultivators typically use fertilizers with a higher nitrogen content to meet the plant's increased demand. Careful monitoring and adjustment of nitrogen levels help prevent deficiencies or excesses, ensuring the plants receive the right balance for optimal vegetative growth.

As cannabis plants transition to the flowering stage, the focus shifts to phosphorus and potassium. Phosphorus plays a crucial role in flower development and overall energy transfer within the plant. It promotes root development, enhances flowering, and produces essential compounds such as adenosine triphosphate (ATP) and nucleic acids. Conversely, potassium supports various physiological processes, including water uptake, enzyme activation, and the synthesis of sugars and starches. Ensuring an appropriate balance of phosphorus and potassium during the flowering stage is vital for developing robust buds and synthesizing cannabinoids and terpenes.

Secondary nutrients, such as calcium (Ca), magnesium (Mg), and sulfur (S), also play essential roles in cannabis cultivation. Calcium is integral to the cell wall structure, providing rigidity and strength to the plant. Magnesium is a central component of chlorophyll, contributing to photosynthesis and overall plant health. Sulfur synthesizes amino acids and proteins essential for various physiological functions. While these secondary nutrients are required in smaller quantities than N-P-K, their availability is crucial for maintaining overall plant vigor and preventing nutrient deficiencies.

Micronutrients, including iron (Fe), manganese (Mn), zinc (Zn), copper (Cu), boron (B), and molybdenum (Mo), are essential for cannabis plants in trace amounts. These micronutrients play diverse roles in enzyme activation, metabolic processes, and overall plant function. Iron, for example, is vital for chlorophyll synthesis, while zinc produces auxins, hormones that regulate plant growth. Copper contributes to lignin formation and helps prevent lodging, supporting plant structure. Boron is crucial for the metabolism of carbohydrates and the development of cell walls. Molybdenum is necessary for nitrogen fixation and overall nitrogen metabolism. While micronutrient deficiencies are less common, maintaining a balanced and well-rounded nutrient regimen ensures that these trace elements are available to the plants when needed.

Various factors, including the pH of the growing medium, influence the availability of nutrients to cannabis plants. pH levels affect nutrient solubility, and maintaining an optimal pH range is crucial for nutrient uptake. Cannabis plants generally prefer a slightly acidic to neutral pH range of 6.0 to 7.0. Deviations from this range can lead to nutrient lockout, where essential nutrients become unavailable to the plants despite being present in the growing medium. If necessary, regular pH testing and adjustment help ensure that the plants can efficiently absorb the nutrients provided.

In soil-based cultivation, organic or synthetic fertilizers are commonly used to meet the nutrient requirements of cannabis plants. Organic fertilizers release nutrients gradually as they decompose, providing a steady and sustainable source of nutrition. Synthetic or mineral-based fertilizers, on the other hand, offer precise control over nutrient concentrations and ratios, allowing cultivators to tailor their feeding regimen to the specific needs of the plants. Hydroponic and soilless growing systems rely on nutrient solutions, where a carefully balanced mix of fertilizers is dissolved in water and delivered directly to the plant roots. Hydroponic systems provide a highly controlled environment, enabling precise adjustments to nutrient levels based on real-time plant needs.

Cannabis cultivators must be attentive to the changing nutrient requirements of plants throughout their life cycle. The vegetative stage demands a higher ratio of nitrogen to support the rapid growth of leaves and branches. Transitioning to the flowering stage necessitates a shift towards phosphorus and potassium to promote the development of buds and flowers. Advanced cultivators may employ nutrient schedules tailored to specific cannabis strains or growing conditions, fine-tuning nutrient concentrations based on the plant's genetics, environmental conditions, and desired outcomes.

Over-fertilization or nutrient excesses can be as detrimental as deficiencies, leading to nutrient burn, where the tips of leaves exhibit signs of stress and discoloration. Careful observation of plant health, including leaf color, size, and overall vigor, helps cultivators identify signs of nutrient imbalances. Adjustments to nutrient concentrations, pH levels, or general feeding practices can then be made in response to the plant's feedback.

Environmental factors, such as temperature, humidity, and light, influence nutrient uptake and metabolism in cannabis plants. Maintaining optimal ecological conditions ensures that plants can effectively utilize the nutrients provided. Temperature extremes can impact the rate of nutrient absorption and enzymatic processes within the plant. High humidity levels may contribute to nutrient deficiencies by limiting transpiration and reducing water uptake and nutrient transport. Adequate lighting, tailored to the plant's specific needs during different stages, enhances photosynthesis and nutrient assimilation.

In conclusion, understanding and managing nutrient requirements are foundational to successful cannabis cultivation. A nuanced approach that considers the varying needs of plants throughout their life cycle, from the early growth stages to the flowering phase, is essential. Cultivators must be attuned to the interplay of primary nutrients, secondary nutrients, and micronutrients, adjusting their feeding regimens based on factors such as plant stage, genetics, and environmental conditions. Regular monitoring, precise nutrient delivery, and a responsive approach to plant health contribute to the overall success of cannabis cultivation, leading to healthy plants, robust yields, and high-quality harvests.

Light and Watering Schedule

The light and watering schedule is a critical component of cannabis cultivation, exerting a profound influence on plant growth, development, and overall health. The interplay between light and water, two fundamental elements for plant life, is carefully orchestrated to mimic natural conditions and optimize the photosynthetic process. Coordinating these schedules is crucial throughout the different stages of the cannabis life cycle, from germination and vegetative growth to flowering and harvest.

Lighting plays a central role in the life of cannabis plants, serving as the energy source for photosynthesis. The amount, intensity, and duration of light exposure significantly impact the plant's metabolic processes, growth patterns, and, ultimately, its yield. In the early growth stages, particularly during germination and the vegetative phase, cannabis plants benefit from an extended light cycle. A common practice is to provide 18 hours of light followed by 6 hours of darkness, creating an environment that encourages robust vegetative growth. High-intensity discharge (HID) lights, fluorescent lights, or light-emitting diodes (LEDs) with a spectrum optimized for vegetative growth are commonly used during this phase. The goal is to simulate the long days of spring and early summer, promoting the development of a strong and well-structured plant.

As cannabis plants transition to the flowering stage, a change in the light cycle is introduced to trigger the reproductive phase. This transition typically involves a shift to a 12-hour light cycle followed by 12 hours of darkness. This simulated autumnal light schedule signals the plants that it is time to focus on flower development. The reduction in the daily light duration mimics the decreasing daylight hours characteristic of the fall season, prompting the plants to allocate energy toward bud formation. Cultivators often deploy bloom-specific lights with a spectrum tailored for flowering during this phase, maximizing the potential for bud production.

Beyond the duration and intensity of light, the quality of light also influences plant development. Different wavelengths of light, commonly referred to as the light spectrum, have varying effects on plant physiology. While blue light encourages vegetative growth and the development of healthy leaves, red light is essential for flowering and overall reproductive processes. Cultivators may adjust the light spectrum during different stages of growth to optimize the desired outcomes. Full-spectrum lights, encompassing a range of wavelengths, offer a balanced approach, providing the broad spectrum of light necessary for the entire cannabis life cycle.

In addition to light, water is a crucial factor in the cultivation equation. Watering practices must be carefully calibrated to ensure optimal hydration without risking overwatering or underwatering, which can harm plant health. The frequency and volume of watering depend on various factors, including the growth stage, environmental conditions, and the plant's specific needs.

During the early growth stages, such as germination and vegetative growth, cannabis plants generally prefer a consistently moist growing medium. This helps ensure that the developing root systems have access to an ample water supply, promoting healthy growth. Care must be taken to avoid waterlogged conditions, as excessive moisture can lead to root rot and other issues. Small, controlled watering sessions are often employed to balance maintaining moisture and preventing wet soil.

As cannabis plants progress to the flowering stage, watering practices may be adjusted to accommodate changing needs. The root systems of flowering plants are often more developed and capable of absorbing larger volumes of water. However, the overall goal remains to maintain a balance, providing adequate moisture without saturating the growing medium. Regularly monitoring the plants' hydration status and attention to environmental factors such as humidity levels guides cultivators in refining their watering practices.

Environmental conditions, including temperature and humidity, also influence the watering schedule. Higher temperatures and lower humidity levels can increase transpiration, increasing water demand. Conversely, cooler temperatures and higher humidity levels may reduce water requirements. Cultivators must adapt their watering schedules based on these environmental dynamics to ensure that the plants receive the appropriate amount of water.

The quality of water used in cultivation is another consideration. Water with a balanced pH and low levels of contaminants is essential for preventing nutrient imbalances and ensuring optimal nutrient uptake. pH levels outside the range of 6.0 to 7.0 can impact nutrient solubility, leading to nutrient deficiencies or excesses. Regular testing and adjustment of water pH contribute to a stable growing environment.

Hydroponic and soilless growing systems introduce a different dimension to watering practices. In these systems, plants are grown in a soilless medium or directly in nutrient-rich water. The nutrient solution is carefully formulated to provide all essential nutrients to the plants' roots. Watering in hydroponic systems involves delivering nutrient solutions, monitoring, and adjustment based on real-time plant needs. This method offers a highly controlled environment, allowing cultivators to tailor nutrient concentrations to the specific requirements of the plants.

The relationship between light and watering schedules is intricately linked to the concept of photoperiodism, the physiological response of plants to the duration of light and darkness. Photoperiod-sensitive cannabis plants rely on the length of the light cycle to initiate flowering. The transition to the flowering stage, triggered by a change in the delicate cycle, influences the plants' water requirements and overall metabolic processes. Cultivators carefully manage both light and watering schedules to synchronize with the natural rhythms of the plants and optimize their growth potential.

Environmental factors, such as the relative humidity of the cultivation space, also influence the interaction between light and water. Higher humidity levels during the early growth stages may impact the transpiration rate and water uptake. In contrast, lower humidity levels during the flowering stage contribute to the prevention of issues such as mold or bud rot. Cultivators may adjust light and watering schedules in response to these environmental dynamics to create an optimal growing environment.

The importance of a well-coordinated light and watering schedule extends beyond the vegetative and flowering stages to the critical period of harvest preparation. As plants mature, cultivators may implement techniques such as flushing, where the plants are rinsed with clean, pH-balanced water without nutrients. This practice aims to remove any residual nutrients from the growing medium and enhance the quality and flavor of the final product. The careful modulation of light and watering schedules during this phase contributes to the development of fully ripened and high-quality buds.

In conclusion, the light and watering schedule is a dynamic and responsive aspect of cannabis cultivation, intricately woven into the fabric of the plant's life cycle. From the extended light cycles that encourage vigorous vegetative growth to the modified light schedules that trigger the flowering phase, cultivators orchestrate a carefully calibrated dance of light exposure. Concurrently, the watering schedule is attuned to the plants' changing needs, adapting to growth stages, environmental conditions, and the overarching goal of promoting health and vitality. The successful cultivation of cannabis hinges on the harmonious integration of light and water, each playing a pivotal role in nurturing the plant from seedling to harvest-ready maturity.

Pruning and Training Techniques

Pruning and training techniques are indispensable tools in the cannabis cultivator's arsenal, offering ways to shape plant growth, optimize light exposure, and ultimately enhance yield and quality. These techniques are particularly crucial during the vegetative phase, where the goal is to encourage a well-structured and bushy plant that can support the weight of mature buds during the flowering stage. Pruning involves the selective removal of specific plant parts, while training techniques manipulate the growth patterns to achieve desired outcomes.

Low-stress training (LST) is a widely employed technique in cannabis cultivation, involving the gentle bending and securing branches to encourage lateral growth. This technique utilizes soft ties or stakes to bend the branches without causing stress or damage. LST is particularly effective in maintaining an even canopy, ensuring all plant parts receive adequate light. By bending branches and exposing more bud sites to direct sunlight, cultivators can promote uniform growth and maximize the potential for bud development. Additionally, LST helps manage the height of the plant, making it suitable for indoor cultivation with limited vertical space.

Topping is another common training technique that involves removing the apical meristem, or the main growth tip, of the plant. This process encourages the development of multiple main colas and effectively divides the plant's energy between several growing tips. Topped plants grow into a bushier shape with more lateral branches, contributing to a more even and robust canopy. Topping is typically performed during the early vegetative stage when the plant has sufficient time to recover and redirect its growth. This technique benefits indoor and outdoor cultivation, allowing cultivators to control the plant's height and shape.

FIMing, an acronym for "f**k, I missed," is a variation of topping that involves removing a portion of the apical meristem instead of the entire tip. This less aggressive approach develops four or more main colas instead of two. FIMing is often favored by cultivators seeking a balance between the increased bud sites achieved through topping and the reduced stress on the plant. Like topping, FIMing is typically performed early in the vegetative stage to allow the plant to recover and redirect its energy toward lateral growth.

Super cropping is a technique that involves gently stressing the plant by bending and partially breaking the stems. This process is performed during the vegetative phase when the stems are still flexible. Super cropping creates strategic weak points in the stems, promoting the formation of additional secondary branches. The benefits of super cropping include improved light penetration, increased bud development, and enhanced overall plant structure. Care must be taken to avoid causing irreversible damage to the stems, and cultivators often use techniques like pinching or rolling rather than outright breaking to achieve the desired results.

Defoliation is a pruning technique involving selective removal of leaves from the plant. While defoliation can be controversial and is not universally applied, proponents argue that it can enhance light penetration, improve air circulation, and redirect energy toward bud development. This technique is typically employed during the vegetative phase and early flowering stage. However, cultivators must exercise caution to avoid excessive stress on the plant, as removing too many leaves can impede its ability to photosynthesize and negatively impact growth.

The application of pruning and training techniques extends into the flowering stage, where the emphasis shifts towards optimizing bud development and maximizing light exposure to bud sites. Strategic defoliation during the early weeks of flowering can help remove unnecessary foliage, allowing more light to reach the developing buds. This practice is often called "lollipopping," as it removes lower leaves and branches, leaving the upper canopy resembling a lollipop shape. Lollipopping concentrates the plant's energy on the upper buds, which receive more direct light and airflow, contributing to higher-quality flowers.

Scrogging, or a green screen, is a training technique that involves using a horizontal screen or net to create an even canopy. Plants are trained to grow horizontally along the screen, ensuring all bud sites receive uniform light exposure. Scrogging is particularly effective in maximizing the potential of indoor cultivation spaces with limited vertical room. By encouraging an even canopy, cultivators can achieve more consistent yields and promote the development of multiple colas.

Main lining, or manifolding, is an advanced training technique that creates a symmetrical plant structure with multiple main colas. This technique begins in the early vegetative stage by strategically pruning and training the plant to develop a symmetrical shape with a specific number of primary branches. The main lining aims to optimize the distribution of energy and nutrients, resulting in larger, more evenly-spaced buds. While this technique requires careful planning and execution, experienced cultivators appreciate its potential for maximizing yields and producing high-quality flowers.

Pruning and training techniques are not limited to indoor cultivation; they can also be applied to outdoor grows. Outdoor cultivators may utilize techniques like topping and LST to manage plant height, enhance light exposure, and encourage lateral growth. These techniques help adapt the plant to the natural environment and promote healthier development. However, outdoor cultivation poses additional challenges, such as variable sunlight and weather conditions, which cultivators must navigate to achieve successful results.

Successful implementation of pruning and training techniques requires understanding the specific needs and characteristics of the cannabis strain being cultivated. Different strains respond differently to these techniques, and cultivators may need to tailor their approach based on genetics, growth patterns, and overall plant vigor.

Also, cultivators must consider the growth stage, environmental conditions, and the desired outcome when deciding which techniques to employ.

While pruning and training techniques offer numerous benefits, cultivators must also be mindful of potential risks and limitations. Overzealous pruning or aggressive training can stress the plant, leading to reduced growth, diminished yields, or even irreversible damage. Careful observation and a gradual approach are crucial to ensuring the plant can adapt and thrive in response to these techniques. Moreover, the plant's overall health, including factors such as nutrient availability, environmental conditions, and disease prevention, must be prioritized alongside pruning and training efforts.

In conclusion, pruning and training techniques are integral components of cannabis cultivation, allowing cultivators to shape plant growth, optimize light exposure, and ultimately improve yields and quality. From low-stress training and topping to super cropping and defoliation, these techniques offer versatile tools for adapting plants to different cultivation environments and achieving specific outcomes. The careful application of pruning and training, tailored to the unique characteristics of each strain and growth stage, contributes to the success of cannabis cultivation, whether indoors or outdoors. As cultivators hone these techniques, they unlock the potential to cultivate healthy, robust plants that produce high-quality flowers with increased potency and desirable characteristics.

CHAPTER V

Transition to Flowering

Recognizing the Flowering Stage

The flowering stage in cannabis cultivation marks a transformative period when the plant transitions from vegetative growth to the production of flowers, ultimately leading to the formation of buds. Recognizing the onset of the flowering stage is crucial for cultivators, as it triggers a shift in care requirements and allows for precise management to optimize yield and quality. This stage is characterized by the emergence of pre-flowers, tiny structures that indicate the plant's sex and signal the impending development of buds. Understanding the key features of the flowering stage, including its duration, environmental considerations, and the plant's nutrient requirements, empowers cultivators to navigate this critical phase successfully.

One of the primary indicators of the flowering stage is the appearance of pre-flowers, typically occurring several weeks after the switch to a 12-hour light cycle. Pre-flowers reveal the plant's gender, distinguishing between male and female plants. Female pre-flowers develop small, hair-like structures called pistils, eventually evolving into characteristic buds. Male pre-flowers, on the other hand, manifest as tiny sacs or balls that contain pollen. Cultivators typically aim to identify and remove male plants promptly, as pollen can lead to undesired pollination, compromising the quality and potency of the harvest.

The timing of the flowering stage varies among cannabis strains, with some entering this phase earlier or later than others. Indica-dominant strains often have a shorter flowering period, typically 7 to 9 weeks, while sativa-dominant strains may require a longer flowering time, up to 12 weeks or more. Hybrid strains exhibit characteristics influenced by indica and sativa genetics, resulting in intermediate flowering durations. Cultivators should consult the breeder's or seed bank's recommendations for each specific strain to accurately anticipate the expected flowering period.

Lighting conditions play a pivotal role in triggering and maintaining the flowering stage. Cannabis plants are photoperiod-sensitive, meaning they respond to changes in the duration of light and darkness. The switch from an 18/6 or 24/0 light cycle (18 hours of light and 6 or 0 hours of darkness) to a 12/12 delicate cycle signals the onset of the flowering stage. Cultivators manipulate the light cycle indoors to induce flowering, while outdoor plants naturally transition as daylight hours decrease with the changing seasons. Maintaining a consistent and uninterrupted 12-hour dark period is crucial, as any light exposure during the dark phase can disrupt the flowering process and potentially lead to stress or hermaphroditism.

As cannabis plants enter the flowering stage, their nutrient requirements shift to accommodate the demands of bud development. While nitrogen remains essential during the early weeks of flowering for sustaining overall plant health, the emphasis transitions to phosphorus and potassium. Phosphorus is a critical component in energy transfer and flower development, while potassium supports essential physiological processes, including water uptake and the synthesis of sugars and starches. Cultivators often switch to a bloom-specific nutrient formula with elevated levels of phosphorus and potassium to meet the plants' changing needs.

Temperature and humidity considerations become increasingly crucial during the flowering stage. Cannabis plants generally thrive between 68-78°F (20-26°C) during the day and slightly cooler temperatures at night. Maintaining these temperature ranges fosters optimal metabolic activity and photosynthesis, promoting healthy bud development. Humidity levels should be carefully managed to prevent issues such as mold or mildew, which can be particularly problematic in the dense buds of flowering plants. Cultivators often gradually decrease humidity levels during the flowering stage to minimize the risk of these moisture-related challenges.

Air circulation and ventilation are essential factors in creating an optimal flowering environment. Proper airflow helps prevent stagnant air pockets, reduces the risk of pests and diseases, and ensures that each bud site receives adequate ventilation. Indoor cultivators may use oscillating fans or other ventilation systems to maintain a consistent and gentle airflow around the plants. Outdoor growers benefit from natural wind movement but may need to assess and enhance airflow in sheltered or densely planted areas.

The development of buds during the flowering stage is a fascinating process marked by distinct phases. Initially, small clusters of pistils emerge at the bud sites, and calyxes begin to swell. Over time, these calyxes become denser and produce trichomes, the resinous glands that contain cannabinoids and terpenes. Trichome development is a crucial aspect of the flowering stage, and the appearance of milky or cloudy trichomes indicates the onset of peak cannabinoid and terpene production. Cultivators often use magnification tools like microscopes or jeweler's loupes to monitor trichome development and determine the optimal harvest time closely.

The later weeks of the flowering stage witness the maturation of trichomes, with a shift from clear to milky or cloudy to amber. The changing color of trichomes corresponds to the evolving cannabinoid profile of the buds. Harvesting during the milky trichome stage generally yields a more uplifting and psychoactive effect, while waiting for amber trichomes may result in a more relaxing and soothing experience. Cultivators may choose the harvest time based on their desired effects, strain characteristics, and individual preferences.

Understanding the signs of peak ripeness and determining the ideal harvest window are critical skills for cultivators seeking to maximize the quality and potency of their buds. Properly cured and dried buds contribute to a smoother smoking experience, enhanced flavor, and improved long-term storage. After harvest, cultivators meticulously trim the buds, removing excess leaves and stems to refine their appearance and optimize cannabinoid concentration. The trimmed buds are then cured in a controlled environment to remove excess moisture, enhance flavor, and preserve potency.

In conclusion, recognizing the flowering stage in cannabis cultivation is essential for cultivators aiming to produce high-quality, potent buds. The transition to flowering is marked by pre-flower emergence and a switch to a 12-hour light cycle, triggering the development of male and female plants. The duration of the flowering stage varies among strains, and careful attention to environmental factors, nutrient requirements, and pest management is crucial for successful cultivation. Monitoring trichome development and choosing the optimal harvest window contribute to the overall quality and effects of the final product. Cultivators who master the intricacies of the flowering stage unlock the potential for bountiful, flavorful, and potent harvests, reaping the rewards of a well-nurtured cannabis cultivation journey.

Adjusting Light Cycles

Adjusting light cycles is a critical aspect of cannabis cultivation, influencing the plant's growth, development, and, ultimately, the quality and yield of the harvest. The manipulation of light cycles is primarily employed to transition the plant between different stages of its life cycle, particularly from the vegetative phase to the flowering stage. Cannabis is a photoperiod-sensitive plant, meaning its physiological processes, including the initiation of flowering, are triggered by changes in the duration of light and darkness. Understanding how and when to adjust light cycles requires a nuanced approach considering factors such as strain genetics, growth objectives, and environmental conditions.

In the vegetative phase, cannabis plants thrive under an extended light cycle, typically 18 hours of light followed by 6 hours of darkness (18/6). This prolonged exposure to light simulates the long spring and early summer days, encouraging robust vegetative growth. During this stage, the plant focuses on developing a solid root system, sturdy stems, and an abundance of healthy leaves. High-intensity discharge (HID) lights, fluorescent lights, or light-emitting diodes (LEDs) with a spectrum optimized for vegetative growth are commonly used to provide the necessary illumination.

The decision to adjust the light cycle and initiate the flowering stage is a pivotal moment in cannabis cultivation. Cultivators often transition to a 12-hour light cycle followed by 12 hours of darkness (12/12) to stimulate the plant's reproductive phase. This light cycle mirrors the natural photoperiod associated with the fall season, signaling the plant that it is time to redirect its energy toward flower development. The timing of this transition depends on various factors, including the strain's genetics, the desired size of the plant, and available cultivation space. Outdoor growers may rely on the changing seasons and decreasing daylight hours to induce flowering naturally. At the same time, indoor cultivators have greater control over the light cycle and can initiate flowering at their discretion.

Indoor cultivators may adjust light cycles gradually or abruptly, depending on their cultivation strategy. Abrupt changes involve an immediate shift from an 18/6 to a 12/12 delicate cycle, signaling a swift transition to the flowering stage. This approach is often favored by cultivators seeking to maximize space utilization and harvest quicker. However, abrupt changes can induce stress in some plants, potentially affecting overall health and yield. Gradual changes, on the other hand, involve incrementally reducing the light cycle over several days or weeks until reaching the desired 12/12 cycle. This gentler approach allows the plant to acclimate to the changing conditions, minimizing stress and promoting a smoother transition.

Outdoor cultivators harness the natural progression of the seasons to guide their plants through the flowering stage. As daylight hours naturally decrease with the approach of fall, cannabis plants receive signals to shift from vegetative growth to flowering. Outdoor cultivation requires careful consideration of the local climate, ensuring that plants have sufficient time to complete the flowering stage before the onset of colder temperatures or frost. Cultivators in regions with unpredictable weather patterns may use supplemental lighting, such as light deprivation techniques, to exert greater control over the flowering initiation.

The implications of adjusting light cycles extend beyond the mere triggering of flowering; they influence the overall structure and characteristics of the plant. A well-timed transition to the flowering stage ensures that the plant has adequate vegetative growth to support the development of robust buds during the flowering phase.

Cultivators often aim for a balanced and uniform canopy, where all plant parts receive consistent light exposure. This contributes to even bud development and facilitates better air circulation, reducing the risk of mold and pest issues.

Light cycles can also be manipulated to achieve specific cultivation goals, such as controlling the height of the plants. Cannabis plants stretch during the early weeks of flowering, particularly during the transition from vegetative growth. Cultivators can use techniques like low-stress training (LST) or a screen of green (Scrog) to manage plant height and create an even canopy. LST involves gently bending and securing branches to encourage lateral growth. At the same time, Scrog employs a horizontal screen to promote an even distribution of light and encourage bud development at multiple sites.

In addition to influencing growth patterns, adjusting light cycles plays a crucial role in determining the potency and effects of the harvested buds. Cannabis plants produce different cannabinoids and terpenes at various life cycle stages, and the light cycle duration during flowering can impact these chemical profiles. Cultivators seeking specific cannabinoid and terpene combinations may experiment with adjusting the delicate cycle and other cultivation practices to achieve the desired outcomes.

The success of adjusting light cycles relies on precise timing and careful observation of the plant's response. The transition to the flowering stage should align with the plant's natural growth patterns and physiological readiness. Cultivators often monitor the plants for signs of pre-flowers, tiny structures that indicate the onset of flowering. Male and female pre-flowers are distinguished, and male plants are typically removed promptly to prevent undesired pollination. Proper timing ensures that the plants enter the flowering stage in optimal health and are well-positioned to produce high-quality buds.

While adjusting light cycles is a powerful tool in cannabis cultivation, it is crucial to strike a balance and avoid unnecessary disruptions. Abrupt changes or frequent alterations to the delicate cycle can induce stress, potentially leading to hermaphroditism, where plants develop both male and female reproductive organs. Stress-induced problems can negatively impact the quality and potency of the final harvest. Cultivators must carefully plan and execute light cycle adjustments based on a thorough understanding of the specific needs of their strains and the desired outcomes of their cultivation efforts.

Environmental factors, such as temperature, humidity, and ventilation, also play a role in the success of adjusting light cycles. Changes in the delicate cycle can influence the overall climate within the cultivation space. Cultivators must ensure that environmental conditions remain within optimal ranges to support healthy growth and prevent heat stress or mold. Adequate ventilation helps maintain a consistent airflow, preventing stagnant air pockets and contributing to overall plant health.

In conclusion, adjusting light cycles is a fundamental and strategic practice in cannabis cultivation, influencing the plant's growth, development, and chemical composition. The transition from an extended vegetative light cycle to a 12/12 light cycle signals the initiation of the flowering stage. This pivotal phase determines the structure and characteristics of the final harvest. Whether indoors or outdoors, cultivators employ various techniques to manipulate light cycles, balancing the need for a smooth transition with the desire to achieve specific cultivation goals. Successful adjustment of light cycles requires careful planning, precise timing, and a comprehensive understanding of the unique characteristics of each strain.

As cultivators master this skill, they unlock the potential to cultivate cannabis plants that thrive in their respective environments and produce high-quality, potent buds with distinct and desirable attributes.

Managing Nutrients for Bud Development

Managing nutrients for bud development is a crucial aspect of cannabis cultivation, where the careful provision of essential elements plays a pivotal role in shaping the harvested buds' size, potency, and overall quality. As cannabis plants progress through their life cycle, transitioning from the vegetative phase to the flowering stage, their nutrient requirements undergo significant shifts. While the vegetative phase emphasizes nitrogen for robust growth, the flowering stage demands a nuanced approach focusing on phosphorus and potassium, essential for flowering and bud development.

During the vegetative phase, cannabis plants exhibit vigorous growth, requiring a balanced nutrient regimen that includes higher levels of nitrogen. Nitrogen is a primary component in chlorophyll, the green pigment responsible for photosynthesis, and supports the development of healthy leaves, stems, and overall plant structure. Cultivators commonly use nitrogen-rich fertilizers during this phase to promote lush, vegetative growth and establish a robust foundation for the impending flowering stage. However, excess nitrogen during the flowering stage can lead to undesirable outcomes, such as delayed bud development and increased susceptibility to certain pests and diseases.

The transition to the flowering stage signals a shift in nutrient priorities, with phosphorus and potassium taking center stage. Phosphorus is a critical element in energy transfer and storage, playing a vital role in synthesizing nucleic acids, ATP (adenosine triphosphate), and other energy-rich molecules. Conversely, potassium contributes to various physiological processes, including water uptake, enzyme activation, and the synthesis of sugars and starches. Together, phosphorus and potassium are essential for developing flowers and producing cannabinoids and terpenes, the compounds responsible for the unique characteristics of cannabis buds.

Cultivators often transition to bloom-specific nutrient formulations designed to meet the plants' changing needs during the flowering stage. These formulations typically contain elevated levels of phosphorus, potassium, and other micronutrients essential for optimal bud development. The precise composition of the nutrient solution may vary based on the specific strain, growing medium, and environmental conditions. Hydroponic systems allow for precise control over nutrient concentrations, enabling cultivators to tailor the nutrient solution to the unique requirements of their plants.

In addition to macronutrients like nitrogen, phosphorus, and potassium, cannabis plants require a range of micronutrients in smaller quantities for healthy growth. Micronutrients, including calcium, magnesium, sulfur, iron, manganese, zinc, copper, and boron, play crucial roles in various physiological processes and enzyme activities. While these essential elements are essential, excessive levels can lead to nutrient imbalances and potential toxicity issues. Cultivators must strike a delicate balance, ensuring that all essential nutrients are available appropriately to support robust bud development without causing adverse effects.

The nutrient delivery method also influences bud development, with different cultivation systems presenting unique considerations. Soil-based cultivation relies on the nutrient content of the growing medium, supplemented by organic or synthetic fertilizers. Cultivators have greater control over nutrient concentrations and delivery in soilless or hydroponic systems, allowing for precise adjustments based on the plants' needs. Hydroponic systems, including deep water culture, nutrient film technique, and aeroponics, provide an oxygen-rich root environment and enhance nutrient uptake efficiency. However, these systems require monitoring and management to prevent nutrient imbalances and ensure optimal delivery.

The timing and frequency of nutrient application are critical considerations in managing nutrients for bud development. Cannabis plants exhibit varying nutrient requirements throughout the flowering stage, with peak demand occurring during the middle to late stages of flower development. Cultivators often follow a feeding schedule that gradually increases nutrient concentrations during the early weeks of flowering, reaching a peak during the bud development phase. Monitoring the plants' response and adjusting nutrient levels based on visual cues, such as leaf color and overall plant health, helps fine-tune the nutrient regimen for optimal results.

Over-fertilization, a common pitfall in nutrient management, can harm bud development. Excessive nutrient concentrations can lead to nutrient burn, where the tips of leaves become discolored and necrotic. This condition not only compromises the plant's overall health but can also impact the quality and potency of the buds. Cultivators must exercise caution in nutrient application, starting with lower concentrations and gradually increasing as the plants progress through the flowering stage. Regular monitoring and adjustments, guided by the plants' responses, contribute to a balanced and effective nutrient management strategy.

The water quality used in nutrient solutions is another critical factor in managing nutrients for bud development. Water with a balanced pH and low levels of contaminants is essential for preventing nutrient lockout and ensuring optimal nutrient uptake by the plants. Cannabis plants prefer a slightly acidic pH range between 6.0 and 7.0, promoting necessary nutrient solubility. Regular monitoring of the water's pH and adjustments as needed contribute to a stable growing environment and help prevent nutrient-related issues.

Organic cultivation practices introduce a different dimension to nutrient management, emphasizing soil health, microbial activity, and organic amendments. Organic fertilizers release nutrients gradually as they break down, providing a sustained and complex nutrient profile. Cultivators may incorporate compost, worm castings, and other organic matter into the soil to enhance microbial diversity and nutrient availability. While organic cultivation offers benefits such as improved soil structure and microbial activity, it requires careful attention to nutrient content and decomposition rates to ensure that plants receive adequate nutrition throughout the flowering stage.

In addition to traditional nutrient management practices, some cultivators explore advanced techniques to optimize bud development further. One such approach is foliar feeding, where nutrient solutions are sprayed directly onto the leaves for rapid absorption. Foliar feeding can effectively address nutrient deficiencies or provide a quick boost during critical growth stages. However, cultivators must exercise caution to avoid applying nutrient solutions during intense light or high-temperature conditions, which can lead to leaf burn.

Microbial inoculants, such as beneficial bacteria and mycorrhizal fungi, are another tool in the arsenal of nutrient management. These microorganisms form symbiotic relationships with the plant roots, enhancing nutrient absorption, disease resistance, and overall plant health. Incorporating microbial inoculants into the cultivation regimen can contribute to a thriving rhizosphere, where beneficial microorganisms work in synergy with the plant to optimize nutrient availability and uptake.

Environmental factors influence nutrient uptake and overall bud development, including temperature, humidity, and airflow. Maintaining optimal ecological conditions ensures that the plants can efficiently utilize nutrients for growth and flower production. High temperatures can increase transpiration rates, leading to an elevated demand for water and nutrients. Conversely, cooler temperatures may slow metabolic processes and nutrient uptake. Humidity levels should be managed to prevent issues such as mold or mildew, which can be particularly problematic in the dense buds of flowering plants.

The final weeks of the flowering stage are critical for nutrient management as cultivators prepare for the harvest phase. Many cultivators implement a process known as flushing, where plants are rinsed with clean, pH-balanced water in the absence of nutrients. Flushing removes residual nutrients from the growing medium, preventing undesirable flavors or harshness in the final product. The flushing duration varies, with some cultivators opting for a short flush period of a few days while others may extend it to one to two weeks. Careful observation of the plants and considerations of strain characteristics and environmental conditions guide cultivators in determining the optimal flushing duration for their specific cultivation context.

In conclusion, managing nutrients for bud development is a nuanced and dynamic aspect of cannabis cultivation, requiring careful consideration of plant needs, environmental factors, and cultivation goals. The transition from the vegetative phase to the flowering stage marks a shift in nutrient priorities, focusing on phosphorus and potassium to support robust flower development. Cultivators must tailor their nutrient regimens to the unique requirements of each strain, adjusting concentrations, timing, and delivery methods based on careful observation and responsive cultivation practices. Whether employing synthetic or organic approaches, cultivators who master nutrient management unlock the potential to cultivate cannabis plants that produce bountiful, potent, and high-quality buds, reflecting the culmination of a well-nurtured cultivation journey.

CHAPTER VI

Pest and Disease Management

Common Pests and Diseases

Common pests and diseases pose significant challenges to cannabis cultivators, threatening the health and vitality of plants and potentially impacting the overall yield and quality of the harvest. Recognizing and effectively managing these issues is an integral aspect of successful cannabis cultivation. Various pests can afflict cannabis plants, ranging from insects to mites, and diseases caused by fungi, bacteria, and viruses further compound the risks. Vigilant monitoring, preventive measures, and prompt intervention are essential components of an integrated pest and disease management strategy.

Insects represent a formidable category of pests that can substantially damage cannabis plants. Aphids, for instance, are small, sap-sucking insects that can increase rapidly and distort the growth of young leaves. Their feeding can lead to stunted plant growth and the transmission of viruses. Spider mites, another common pest, are microscopic arachnids that feed on plant sap, causing discoloration and stippling on leaves. These pests are particularly challenging to manage due to their rapid reproduction and ability to develop resistance to pesticides. Thrips, tiny winged insects, can cause damage by scraping the surface of leaves and leaving behind scars. Their feeding may lead to distorted growth, discoloration, and the transmission of plant viruses. Whiteflies are another notorious pest that can impact cannabis cultivation. These tiny, winged insects feed on plant sap and excrete honeydew, fostering the growth of sooty mold. Whiteflies can transmit plant viruses and weaken the overall health of cannabis plants. Fungus gnats, small flying insects, pose different challenges by infesting the soil and laying eggs near the plant's root zone. The larvae feed on root hairs, leading to nutrient uptake issues and weakened plant vigor. Controlling insect pests often involves a combination of cultural practices, such as maintaining a clean and sanitary growing environment and the targeted use of insecticides or biological controls.

Beyond insect pests, cannabis plants are susceptible to various diseases caused by fungi, bacteria, and viruses. Powdery mildew is a prevalent fungal disease that manifests as a white, powdery substance on leaves and stems. It thrives in conditions of high humidity and can severely impact bud quality. Downy mildew, another fungal pathogen, appears as yellow or brown spots on leaves and can lead to the development of fuzzy, purplish spores on the undersides of leaves. Root rot, caused by various fungi, can occur in waterlogged or poorly drained soil, leading to the decay of the plant's root system and a decline in overall health.

Bacterial infections also pose significant risks to cannabis cultivation. Bacterial leaf spots, characterized by dark lesions with yellow halos, can spread rapidly and compromise leaf function. Crown gall, caused by the bacterium Agrobacterium tumefaciens, forms swollen growths or galls on stems and roots, affecting nutrient and water transport. Erwinia, another bacterial pathogen, can cause soft rot and tissue breakdown in various plant parts.

Viruses present an additional set of challenges for cannabis cultivators. Tobacco mosaic virus (TMV) and cucumber mosaic virus (CMV) are among the viruses that can infect cannabis plants, leading to symptoms such as mosaic patterns, leaf distortion, and stunted growth. These viruses are often transmitted by insects, emphasizing the interconnected nature of pest and disease management.

Integrated pest management (IPM) is a holistic approach that combines various strategies to prevent and control pests and diseases. Cultural practices, such as maintaining a clean and well-ventilated growing environment, are foundational to IPM. Regularly monitoring plants for signs of pests or diseases allows for early detection and intervention. Beneficial insects, such as ladybugs and predatory mites, can be introduced to the cultivation space to control pest populations naturally. Additionally, neem oil, insecticidal soaps, and other biopesticides provide alternative, less harmful options for pest control.

Quarantine measures are crucial in preventing the introduction and spread of pests and diseases. New plants or clones should be thoroughly inspected before being introduced to the cultivation area to avoid bringing in potential contaminants. Strict sanitation practices, including cleaning tools, equipment, and grow spaces, help eliminate possible breeding grounds for pests and pathogens. The use of disease-resistant cannabis cultivars, when available, provides an additional layer of protection against certain pests and diseases.

Chemical pesticides can be practical tools in pest and disease management, but their use requires careful consideration. Selective pesticides that target specific pests or diseases minimize the impact on beneficial organisms and reduce the risk of developing pesticide resistance. Rotating or alternating between different classes of pesticides can also help prevent resistance. Cultivators must adhere to proper application rates, timing, and safety precautions when using chemical pesticides to avoid adverse effects on the plants, the environment, and human health.

Preventive measures, including proper plant nutrition and stress management, contribute to the resilience of cannabis plants against pests and diseases. Healthy plants with robust immune systems are better equipped to withstand potential threats. Ensuring optimal growing conditions, including appropriate watering practices and well-balanced nutrient regimens, fosters plant vigor and reduces susceptibility to stress-related issues.

The importance of early detection must be considered in pest and disease management. Regular scouting of plants for signs of pests, such as distorted leaves, stippling, discoloration, or the presence of insects, allows for swift intervention before infestations escalate. Similarly, monitoring for symptoms of diseases, including abnormal spots, lesions, or unusual growth patterns, enables timely diagnosis and treatment.

When pests or diseases are identified, targeted and appropriate intervention strategies must be implemented promptly. Biological controls, such as the release of predatory insects or the application of beneficial microbes, offer environmentally friendly options for pest management. Cultural practices, such as removing and destroying infected plant material, help prevent the spread of diseases within the cultivation space. Quarantine measures may involve isolating affected plants to prevent the spreading of pests or diseases.

While proactive management strategies are essential, cultivators should be prepared to address unexpected pest or disease outbreaks. A contingency plan outlining specific actions during an infestation or disease outbreak ensures a swift and organized response. This plan may include the availability of appropriate pesticides, the contact information of pest control professionals, and steps to mitigate the spread of pests or diseases.

Regular education and training for cultivators on pest and disease management practices contribute to a proactive and informed approach. Understanding common pests' life cycles, behaviors, and vulnerabilities allows cultivators to implement targeted and effective control measures. Similarly, staying knowledgeable about emerging pests and diseases within the cannabis industry enables cultivators to adapt their management strategies accordingly.

Environmental controls, including temperature, humidity, and ventilation, play a role in preventing and managing pests and diseases. Maintaining optimal conditions discourages the proliferation of certain pests and pathogens. Adequate ventilation helps reduce humidity levels, mitigating the risk of issues such as powdery mildew. Implementing temperature controls can deter specific pests' activity or slow the development of certain diseases.

Research and development in cannabis cultivation continue to contribute to innovative pest and disease management solutions. Cultivators benefit from staying informed about the latest advancements, including new biological controls, resistant cultivars, and sustainable practices. Collaborating with experts, attending industry conferences, and participating in online forums provide avenues for cultivators to share knowledge and learn from the experiences of others in the field.

In conclusion, effectively managing common pests and diseases is paramount for successful cannabis cultivation. A comprehensive and integrated approach, encompassing cultural practices, preventive measures, early detection, and targeted interventions, is essential for minimizing the impact of pests and diseases on plant health and overall crop quality. The interconnected nature of pest and disease management underscores the importance of a holistic perspective that considers diverse threats and leverages various strategies to ensure a resilient and thriving cannabis cultivation environment. By adopting proactive and informed practices, cultivators can safeguard their crops, optimize yields, and contribute to the sustainability and success of the cannabis industry.

Prevention Strategies

Prevention strategies are foundational to the success of cannabis cultivation, serving as a proactive approach to safeguarding plants against potential threats, including pests, diseases, and environmental stressors. A comprehensive prevention strategy involves a combination of cultural practices, stringent sanitation measures, and environmental controls to create an optimal growing environment for cannabis plants. By minimizing risks and creating conditions conducive to plant health, cultivators can reduce the likelihood of issues arising throughout the cultivation cycle, ultimately leading to healthier plants, improved yields, and enhanced overall crop quality.

Cultural practices form the backbone of prevention strategies, emphasizing the implementation of techniques that promote plant health and vitality. The use of disease-resistant cannabis cultivars is a fundamental aspect of this approach. Cultivators should select strains that exhibit natural resistance or tolerance to common pests and diseases in their cultivation environment. Resistant cultivars provide an added layer of protection, reducing the likelihood of infestations or infections and minimizing the need for intensive pest management measures. Maintaining a clean and sanitized cultivation space is paramount to preventing the introduction and spread of pests and diseases. Regular removal of plant debris, fallen leaves, and other organic matter eliminates potential habitats for pests and pathogens. Infected or infested plant material should be promptly removed and destroyed to prevent the spreading of diseases or pests within the cultivation area. Sanitation measures extend to regularly cleaning and disinfecting tools, equipment, and surfaces to minimize contamination risk.

Quarantine procedures play a crucial role in preventing the introduction of pests and diseases to the cultivation space. New plants or clones should be thoroughly inspected and quarantined before being integrated into the main cultivation area. This precautionary measure allows cultivators to identify potential issues early on and prevent the accidental introduction of pests or diseases that may have been present in new plant material.

Temperature and humidity management are vital components of prevention strategies. Maintaining optimal environmental conditions discourages the proliferation of certain pests and pathogens. High humidity levels can create favorable conditions for issues like powdery mildew, while excessively low humidity may lead to problems like spider mite infestations. Proper ventilation and airflow contribute to a healthy growing environment, reducing the risk of stagnant air pockets and promoting transpiration, which helps deter certain pests.

Integrated pest management (IPM) is a holistic approach incorporating preventive measures into the overall cultivation strategy. By employing beneficial insects or predatory organisms that naturally control pest populations, cultivators enhance the resilience of their crops against potential threats. Ladybugs, predatory mites, and nematodes are beneficial organisms that can be introduced to the cultivation space to maintain a balanced ecosystem and mitigate the impact of pests.

Preventive spraying of horticultural oils or insecticidal soaps can create a protective barrier on plant surfaces and deter certain pests. These products are less harmful to beneficial insects and can be part of a proactive strategy to prevent pest infestations. Neem oil, derived from the neem tree, is another natural product with insecticidal and antifungal properties, making it a valuable tool in prevention strategies.

Crop rotation is an agricultural practice that involves changing the type of crop grown in a particular area from one season to the next. In cannabis cultivation, rotating crops can help break the life cycle of pests or diseases that may be specific to cannabis. This practice is particularly relevant for outdoor or greenhouse cultivators with larger cultivation areas, allowing them to disrupt the reproduction and survival of pests or pathogens that rely on a continuous host.

Preventive measures extend to the proper management of irrigation practices. Overwatering can create conditions conducive to root rot, a common issue that affects the root system of cannabis plants. Ensuring that plants receive adequate water without promoting waterlogged soil is crucial for preventing root-related problems. Well-draining growing mediums and attentive irrigation practices contribute to maintaining an optimal balance of moisture in the root zone.

Nutrient management is an integral part of prevention strategies, influencing the overall health and resilience of cannabis plants. Providing plants with a well-balanced nutrient regimen supports robust growth and enhances their ability to withstand stressors. Over-fertilization can lead to nutrient imbalances and potential toxicity issues, while under-fertilization may result in nutrient deficiencies, weakening the plants' immune systems. Monitoring nutrient levels, adjusting formulations based on plant needs, and adhering to proper application rates contribute to a proactive nutrient management approach.

A strict routine inspection and monitoring schedule is crucial for early detection and intervention. Regularly examining plants for signs of stress, discoloration, pest damage, or disease symptoms allows cultivators to identify issues in their early stages. Swift action can then be taken to address problems before they escalate. Utilizing magnification tools, such as microscopes or jeweler's loupes, during inspections allows for a closer examination of plant surfaces and aids in the early identification of pests or diseases.

Environmental controls, such as physical barriers, can contribute to prevention strategies. Installing barriers like row covers or netting in outdoor cultivation can deter certain pests and protect plants from external threats. Similarly, using screens or filters on intake vents in indoor cultivation spaces helps prevent the entry of airborne pests. Controlling access points and securing the cultivation area minimize the risk of external contamination.

Education and training are essential components of effective prevention strategies. Cultivators and cultivation staff should be well-informed about the specific pests and diseases that may affect cannabis plants in their region. Understanding common threats' life cycles, behaviors, and vulnerabilities allows for developing targeted and informed prevention measures. Training programs and regular updates on emerging pests or diseases contribute to a knowledgeable and proactive cultivation team.

In conclusion, prevention strategies form the cornerstone of successful cannabis cultivation, emphasizing proactive measures to create a robust and resilient growing environment. Cultural practices, sanitation measures, environmental controls, and integrated pest management techniques collectively contribute to minimizing risks and optimizing plant health. By adopting a comprehensive and vigilant approach to prevention, cultivators can reduce the likelihood of issues arising, ensuring healthier plants, higher yields, and enhanced overall crop quality. The cultivation of cannabis becomes a sustainable and successful endeavor when prevention strategies are integrated into every stage of the cultivation cycle, reflecting a commitment to plant health and the long-term viability of the cannabis industry.

Organic Pest Control Methods

Organic pest control methods are gaining prominence in cannabis cultivation as cultivators increasingly prioritize sustainable and environmentally friendly practices. These methods focus on harnessing the power of nature to manage pest populations while minimizing the use of synthetic pesticides that can harm beneficial organisms, the ecosystem, and, potentially, the end product. Organic pest control aligns with the principles of organic farming, emphasizing a holistic and integrated approach that prioritizes soil health, biodiversity, and overall ecosystem balance.

One of the fundamental strategies in organic pest control is using beneficial insects. Predatory insects, such as ladybugs, lacewings, and predatory mites, are crucial in controlling pest populations. Ladybugs, for example, are voracious consumers of aphids, mites, and other soft-bodied pests. Introducing these beneficial insects to the cultivation space creates a natural and sustainable pest control method. These predators balance the ecosystem by preying on harmful pests and preventing infestations without chemical interventions.

Neem oil, derived from the neem tree (Azadirachta indica), is a widely used organic pest control method. It contains compounds that act as insecticides, disrupting various pests' feeding, development, and reproduction. Neem oil is effective against multiple pests, including aphids, spider mites, whiteflies, and caterpillars. Its organic nature makes it a preferred choice for cultivators aiming to minimize the impact of chemical pesticides on the environment. However, it's essential to note that neem oil should be applied judiciously, as excessive use may lead to issues such as leaf burn.

Introducing predatory nematodes to the growing medium is another organic method of controlling soil-dwelling pests. These microscopic roundworms, specifically Steinernema and Heterorhabditis species, seek out and parasitize pests like fungus gnats and certain beetle larvae. Nematodes are a valuable addition to organic pest control regimens, particularly in soil-based cultivation, as they provide targeted control without harming beneficial organisms or affecting the overall ecosystem.

Companion planting, a practice rooted in agroecology, involves strategically placing plants that deter pests or attract beneficial insects near cannabis crops. Certain plants, such as marigolds, basil, and mint, emit natural compounds that repel pests. Integrating these companion plants into the cultivation area creates a natural barrier against unwanted insects. Additionally, flowering plants like yarrow and dill attract pollinators and beneficial insects, contributing to a diverse and balanced ecosystem that supports natural pest control.

Diatomaceous earth is a versatile and organic substance derived from fossilized diatoms. It consists of microscopic, sharp-edged particles that effectively dehydrate and kill insects. When applied to the soil or directly on plant surfaces, diatomaceous earth acts as a physical barrier against crawling pests. It is beneficial for controlling pests like ants, beetles, and caterpillars. Diatomaceous earth is non-toxic to humans and animals, making it a safe and environmentally friendly choice for organic pest control.

Incorporating insecticidal soaps into an organic pest control strategy effectively manages soft-bodied pests such as aphids, mites, and whiteflies. These soaps, typically made from potassium salts of fatty acids, disrupt insects' cell membranes upon contact, leading to dehydration and eventual demise. Insecticidal soaps are considered low-risk to beneficial insects, mammals, and birds, making them suitable for integrated pest management in organic cultivation.

Biological insecticides, derived from naturally occurring microorganisms, are increasingly popular in organic pest control. Bacillus thuringiensis (Bt) is a bacterial insecticide widely used to combat caterpillar pests. When applied, it produces toxic proteins in specific insect larvae, providing targeted control without harming other organisms. Another example is spinosad, derived from soil bacteria, which targets a broad spectrum of pests, including thrips, caterpillars, and beetles. These biological insecticides are effective, have minimal impact on non-target organisms, and break down quickly in the environment.

Using pheromones for pest control has gained traction in organic cultivation. Pheromones are chemicals produced by insects to communicate with each other. In pest management, synthetic pheromones can disrupt the mating patterns of specific pests, leading to reduced reproduction and population control. This approach, known as mating disruption, offers a targeted and environmentally friendly solution, minimizing the need for chemical pesticides.

Organic fungicides prevent and manage fungal diseases without resorting to synthetic chemicals. Copper-based fungicides, such as copper sulfate or copper hydroxide, are commonly used in organic cultivation to control diseases like powdery mildew and downy mildew. These fungicides disrupt the cell membranes of fungal spores, preventing their germination and spread. While copper-based fungicides are effective, careful application and monitoring are essential to avoid copper accumulation in the soil.

Implementing crop rotation as an organic pest control method helps disrupt the life cycles of pests and diseases. By changing the type of crop planted in a specific area each season, cannabis cultivators can reduce the build-up of pests or pathogens that may be specific to cannabis. Crop rotation contributes to overall soil health, enhances biodiversity, and creates an inhospitable environment for pests adapted to particular host plants.

Organic soil amendments, such as compost and well-aged manure, contribute to soil health and resilience, creating conditions that discourage pests and diseases. Healthy soil supports a robust microbial community and enhances nutrient availability for plants. Additionally, certain amendments, like garlic or hot pepper-based solutions, can act as natural repellents against pests when incorporated into the soil or used as foliar sprays.

Implementing cultural practices that promote plant health is integral to organic pest control. Providing optimal growing conditions, including appropriate watering, well-balanced nutrient regimens, and proper spacing between plants, contributes to plant vigor and resilience. Strong and healthy plants are better equipped to withstand pest pressure and are less susceptible to infestations or diseases.

Encouraging biodiversity within the cultivation area is a fundamental principle of organic pest control. A diverse ecosystem with various plant species attracts beneficial insects, birds, and other organisms, contributing to natural pest management. Cultivators may incorporate hedgerows, cover crops, or native vegetation to enhance biodiversity and create habitats for natural predators.

Regular monitoring and early intervention are crucial to any organic pest control strategy. Regularly inspecting plants for signs of pests, diseases, or stress allows cultivators to identify issues in their early stages. Timely intervention, whether through the release of beneficial insects, organic treatments, or cultural practices, prevents the escalation of problems and supports a proactive approach to pest control.

Educating cultivation staff about organic pest control methods and the importance of a holistic approach contributes to the success of these practices. Training programs that emphasize the identification of beneficial insects, understanding the life cycles of pests, and implementing preventive measures empower cultivators to make informed decisions in their pest management strategies.

In conclusion, organic pest control methods embody a sustainable and environmentally conscious approach to managing pests in cannabis cultivation. Cultivators can create resilient and thriving cultivation environments by leveraging nature's power through beneficial insects, organic treatments, and cultural practices. These methods align with the principles of organic farming, emphasizing the interconnectedness of soil health, biodiversity, and overall ecosystem balance. Organic pest control addresses immediate pest concerns and fosters a long-term commitment to sustainability, promoting the health of both the plants and the surrounding environment.

CHAPTER VII

Harvesting and Curing

Determining the Right Harvest Time

Determining the right harvest time is a critical decision in cannabis cultivation, influencing the potency, flavor, and overall quality of the final product. Various factors influence the optimal harvest window, and cultivators must carefully assess the readiness of their plants to achieve the desired characteristics in the harvested buds. From the onset of flowering to the final days before harvest, cannabis plants undergo significant changes, and timing is crucial to capture the peak levels of cannabinoids, terpenes, and other compounds that contribute to the unique attributes of each strain.

The flowering phase marks a transformative period in the cannabis life cycle, characterized by the development of resinous buds containing cannabinoids, such as THC (tetrahydrocannabinol) and CBD (cannabidiol), along with an array of aromatic terpenes. Understanding the progression of the flowering stage is essential for determining the right harvest time. Most cannabis strains have an approximate flowering time ranging from 6 to 12 weeks, though individual variations can occur. The breeder's specifications and strain characteristics guide cultivators on when to expect the onset of flowering and subsequent maturation.

Visual cues play a significant role in gauging the readiness of cannabis plants for harvest. Trichomes, the tiny, mushroom-shaped structures covering the surfaces of buds and leaves, are critical indicators of cannabinoid and terpene development. As plants mature, trichomes change color, typically transitioning from clear to cloudy and, in some cases, to amber. The trichome coloration is closely associated with cannabinoid content, with clear trichomes indicating early stages of development, cloudy trichomes signifying peak potency, and amber trichomes suggesting a potential degradation of cannabinoids into CBN (cannabinol), associated with a more soothing effect.

Examining trichomes with a magnifying tool, such as a jeweler's loupe or a microscope, allows cultivators to accurately observe the trichome heads' color and clarity. While individual preferences may vary, many cultivators aim for a harvest window when most trichomes are cloudy, which is often associated with the peak of cannabinoid production. The appearance of amber trichomes may signal that the plants have surpassed their prime, with THC content starting to degrade. The careful observation of trichomes is a skill cultivated through experience and serves as a valuable tool for precision in determining the ideal harvest time.

Beyond trichome examination, observing the overall maturity and appearance of the cannabis buds provides additional insights. Mature buds generally exhibit swelling and denseness, with fully formed calyxes and abundant resin. The coloration of pistils and the hair-like structures covering the buds can also indicate harvest readiness. During the flowering phase, pistils typically change from white to darker, such as orange or brown, though this alone is not a foolproof indicator. A combination of visual cues, including trichome color and overall bud development, contributes to a more comprehensive assessment of the optimal harvest window.

The consideration of strain-specific characteristics is crucial when determining the right harvest time. Indica and Sativa strains and hybrid varieties may exhibit distinct growth patterns and maturation timelines. Indica- dominant strains often have a shorter flowering period and may reach maturity sooner than Sativa-dominant strains, which tend to have a more extended flowering phase. Additionally, the specific genetics of a strain influence factors such as bud structure, terpene profiles, and cannabinoid ratios. Cultivators should reference breeder or strain-specific guidelines and factor in these genetic nuances when making harvest decisions.

Cultivators may also choose to monitor the changes in aroma and flavor as part of the harvest determination process. As cannabis plants mature, the terpene profile evolves, contributing to the distinctive scent and taste of the buds. Harvesting during the terpene development peak can enhance the final product's aromatic and gustatory qualities. Cultivators who prioritize terpene preservation may opt for a harvest time that aligns with the desired flavor profile, even if cannabinoid levels have not reached their absolute peak.

Environmental conditions and the overall health of the plants play a significant role in determining the right harvest time. Adverse conditions, such as pest infestations, nutrient deficiencies, or extreme weather events, can impact the maturation process and compromise the quality of the buds. A stressed plant may exhibit premature senescence and age and mature more rapidly than under optimal conditions. Conversely, a healthy and well-nurtured plant is more likely to follow its natural maturation timeline, allowing for the full expression of cannabinoids and terpenes.

Cultivators often utilize a flush period in the pre-harvest phase to improve the quality of the final product. Flushing involves irrigating the plants with clean, pH-balanced water without nutrients for a specified duration before harvest. This process removes residual nutrients from the growing medium, preventing undesirable flavors or harshness in the buds. Flushing duration may vary, with some cultivators opting for a shorter flush of a few days while others may extend it to one to two weeks. The decision to flush and the duration chosen depend on factors such as the cultivation medium, nutrient regimen, and strain characteristics.

The consideration of cannabinoids, terpenes, and other compounds is about achieving peak potency and tailoring the final product's effects to meet specific preferences or medicinal needs. The interplay between cannabinoids, primarily THC and CBD, along with the diverse array of terpenes, contributes to the unique experiences associated with different strains. Cultivators may have specific goals in mind, such as maximizing THC content for recreational strains or achieving a balanced CBD-to-THC ratio for medicinal purposes. Understanding the desired cannabinoid and terpene profile guides the cultivator in selecting the optimum harvest time to align with these goals.

In the context of medical cannabis, the harvest time is particularly crucial, as it directly impacts the therapeutic properties of the final product. Patients seeking specific therapeutic effects, such as pain relief, anti-anxiety properties, or anti-inflammatory benefits, may benefit from a targeted approach to harvest timing. For instance, strains with higher levels of CBD may be harvested later to ensure the development of this non-psychoactive cannabinoid associated with various therapeutic properties.

Cultivators may also implement staggered harvesting, particularly in more extensive cultivation operations where multiple plants or batches may have different maturation timelines. Staggered harvesting involves selectively harvesting individual plants or canopy sections based on readiness. This approach allows cultivators to capture the peak maturation of each plant or section and optimize the overall quality of the harvest.

Post-harvest considerations are integral to the determination of the right harvest time. Once the plants are harvested, the drying and curing processes significantly influence the final product's quality, potency, and overall experience. Properly drying and curing cannabis buds involves carefully controlling environmental conditions, such as temperature and humidity, to preserve cannabinoids, terpenes, and moisture content. Rushing or neglecting these post-harvest steps can diminish the full potential of the harvest, impacting flavor, aroma, and overall enjoyment. In conclusion, determining the right harvest time in cannabis cultivation is a nuanced and multifaceted decision that requires a combination of factors. From the visual examination of trichomes and overall bud development to considering strain-specific characteristics, environmental conditions, and post-harvest goals, cultivators must navigate a dynamic process to optimize the quality and potency of their final product. The art and science of determining the right harvest time reflect the culmination of a cultivator's experience, knowledge, and ability to adapt to the unique characteristics of each cannabis strain. By honing these skills, cultivators can consistently produce cannabis buds that not only meet but exceed the expectations of consumers and patients alike.

Harvesting Techniques

Harvesting techniques in cannabis cultivation are pivotal in ensuring the successful culmination of a growth cycle, with careful timing and precise methods influencing the quality, potency, and overall characteristics of the harvested buds. The culmination of weeks or months of cultivation efforts comes to fruition during the harvest, where cultivators employ various techniques to harvest mature cannabis plants delicately and efficiently. This critical phase involves not only the physical removal of the plant material but also the consideration of factors such as timing, trimming, and post-harvest handling, all of which contribute to the ultimate quality of the end product.

Timing is paramount in harvesting cannabis plants, and it aligns closely with the maturity of the trichomes, the microscopic resin glands that house cannabinoids and terpenes. As cultivators monitor the progression of flowering, they pay particular attention to the trichomes' coloration, transitioning from clear to cloudy and potentially to amber. The dirty trichome stage is often associated with peak cannabinoid content, while amber trichomes may indicate a degradation of THC into CBN. Cultivators typically aim to harvest when most trichomes are cloudy, representing an optimal balance between peak potency and the preservation of desirable terpenes. The choice between harvesting the entire plant at once or employing a staggered or selective harvesting approach depends on factors such as cultivation scale, strain characteristics, and growth patterns. Staggered harvesting involves selectively harvesting individual plants or specific canopy sections based on readiness. This method allows cultivators to capture the peak maturation of each plant or section, optimizing overall quality. In contrast, harvesting the entire crop at once may be more suitable for smaller operations or strains with uniform maturation, simplifying the logistics of harvest and post-harvest processes.

When the decision is made to proceed with harvesting, the method employed for plant removal is crucial. Cultivators commonly use a combination of pruning shears or scissors to cut individual branches or the entire plant. Precision is critical to avoid damaging the delicate trichomes and to facilitate efficient post-harvest handling. The use of clean and sharp cutting tools is essential to minimize stress on the plants and reduce the risk of introducing contaminants.

Some cultivators opt for a wet trim, where the large fan leaves and excess foliage are removed immediately after harvest. In contrast, others prefer a dry trim, deferring the trimming process until after drying. Personal preferences, cultivation practices, and the drying environment often influence the choice between wet and dry trimming. Wet trimming may expedite drying but requires meticulous attention to prevent mold or mildew growth. Dry trimming allows for a slower, more controlled drying process but may be labor-intensive.

The post-harvest handling of cannabis plants significantly impacts the final product's quality. Immediately after harvest, the plants undergo a drying phase to reduce moisture content, preserve cannabinoids and terpenes, and prevent mold or mildew development. Proper drying involves maintaining a controlled environment with adequate ventilation, moderate temperature, and relative humidity. Cultivators often hang individual branches or entire plants upside down in a dark and well-ventilated space to promote even drying.

The duration of the drying phase varies but typically lasts 7 to 14 days. Cultivators monitor the progress by checking the stems' snap consistency, with a desirable sound indicating an adequately dried plant. Over-drying should be avoided, as it can lead to harshness in the final product, while under-drying may pose risks of mold development during subsequent storage.

Following the drying phase, cannabis buds undergo curing, a process that further refines their characteristics. Curing involves placing dried buds in airtight containers, commonly glass jars, to allow for the slow release of remaining moisture and the development of desired flavors, aromas, and smoothness. The curing period typically spans several weeks to a few months, with cultivators burping the containers periodically to release built-up gases and promote optimal conditions.

Harvesting techniques extend beyond the physical removal and post-harvest handling of plants; they also encompass the trimming process, which plays a crucial role in refining the appearance and marketability of the final product. Trimming involves the removal of excess foliage, fan leaves, and stems, focusing on the manicuring of the buds to enhance their visual appeal. Trimming can be performed during or after the drying phase, depending on the chosen method (wet or dry trimming) and individual preferences.

The choice between machine trimming and hand trimming is a consideration that cultivators face, each method carrying its advantages and drawbacks. Machine trimming offers efficiency, especially for large-scale operations, but may need to be more precise and may generate more trim material. Hand trimming, while labor-intensive, allows for meticulous attention to detail, ensuring a polished and visually appealing final product. Some cultivators may combine both methods, using machines for bulk trimming and hand finishing for premium or boutique strains.

The aesthetic quality of the trimmed buds is a significant factor in consumer preference and market competitiveness. Well-trimmed buds enhance visual appeal and contribute to a smoother smoking experience, as excess plant material can impart undesirable flavors or harshness. Trimmers must delicately navigate the contours of each bud, removing unwanted material while preserving the integrity of the trichomes and resinous surfaces.

Beyond the visual aspects, trimming also influences the market presentation of cannabis products. The decision to present buds in their whole form or to break them down into smaller, more manageable units, such as pre-rolls or pre-packaged flowers, reflects market trends and consumer preferences. The manicuring of buds and the packaging presentation contribute to a cultivator's products' overall branding and market positioning. Post-harvest handling also extends to the storage and preservation of the final product. Proper storage conditions are crucial to maintaining the buds' quality over time, preventing degradation of cannabinoids, terpenes, and overall potency. Cultivators often store cured buds in a cool, dark, and airtight environment, such as glass jars or vacuum-sealed packaging, to minimize exposure to light, air, and temperature fluctuations.

Quality control measures are integral to harvesting techniques, ensuring the final product meets established standards for potency, cleanliness, and overall quality. Cultivators may implement testing protocols, including laboratory analysis for cannabinoid and terpene profiles and screening for contaminants such as pesticides, molds, or residual solvents. Rigorous quality control measures contribute to consumer safety, regulatory compliance, and the cultivator's reputation within the industry.

In conclusion, harvesting techniques in cannabis cultivation encompass a series of strategic decisions and precise actions that significantly impact the final product's quality, potency, and market presentation. From the critical timing of the harvest based on trichome maturity to the careful removal of plants and the meticulous trimming process, cultivators navigate a dynamic and multifaceted process. Post-harvest handling, including drying, curing, and storage, further refines the characteristics of the buds. The interplay of these techniques influences the immediate consumer experience and establishes the cultivator's reputation and positioning within the competitive cannabis market. By mastering the art and science of harvesting techniques, cultivators can consistently produce cannabis products that meet or exceed consumers' expectations and contribute to the success of their cultivation endeavors.

Proper Drying and Curing Methods

Proper drying and curing methods are crucial stages in the post-harvest process of cannabis cultivation, playing a pivotal role in preserving the quality, potency, and overall characteristics of the harvested buds. These techniques are essential for achieving a smooth, flavorful end product that meets consumer expectations and regulatory standards. The drying and curing phases are intricate processes that require careful attention to environmental conditions, timing, and the cultivator's expertise to unlock the full potential of the harvested cannabis.

The drying phase is the initial step after harvest, and its primary objective is to reduce the moisture content in the buds. Effective drying not only prevents the development of mold and mildew but also sets the stage for the subsequent curing process. Cultivators must strike a delicate balance during this phase, aiming to remove excess moisture without over-drying the buds, which could result in a harsh and unpleasant smoking experience.

A controlled drying environment is essential for preserving cannabinoids, terpenes, and other volatile compounds while minimizing the risk of degradation. Cultivators commonly hang harvested branches or plants upside down in a dark, well-ventilated space. The drying room should maintain a moderate temperature, ideally around 60 to 70 degrees Fahrenheit (15 to 21 degrees Celsius), with a relative humidity level between 45% and 55%. Adequate airflow is crucial to ensure even drying and prevent mold formation.

The duration of the drying phase varies but typically lasts 7 to 14 days. Throughout this period, cultivators monitor the progress by assessing the snap consistency of the stems. Buds should be dry enough to snap off the stems with a crisp sound, indicating an adequately dried plant. Over-drying should be avoided, as it can lead to a harsh taste and diminished aromatic qualities. Conversely, under-drying increases the risk of mold growth during subsequent storage.

Properly dried cannabis buds then enter the curing phase, a process that refines their characteristics, enhances flavor, and improves overall quality. Curing involves placing dried buds in airtight containers, usually glass jars, to allow for the slow release of remaining moisture. This controlled environment encourages the development of desirable flavors and aromas and a smoother smoking experience. The curing period typically spans several weeks to a few months, during which cultivators "burp" the containers periodically to release built-up gases and promote optimal conditions.

The curing process is akin to aging wine or cheese, allowing time for the chemical reactions within the buds to continue. During curing, chlorophyll breaks down, producing a milder taste and smoother smoke. Additionally, terpenes, the aromatic compounds responsible for the diverse scents in cannabis, undergo changes that contribute to developing unique flavors. Proper curing can transform a somewhat grassy or herbal taste into a more nuanced and enjoyable palate.

Cultivators often monitor humidity levels within the curing containers, aiming for a 55% to 65% range. Too high humidity may lead to mold, while overly dry conditions can compromise the curing process. The goal is to achieve an equilibrium that facilitates the slow release of moisture from the bud without allowing it to become scorched or lose its aromatic qualities.

Curing also involves rotating the buds within the containers, ensuring even exposure to air, and promoting consistent curing throughout the entire batch. Regularly inspecting the buds during the curing process allows cultivators to identify potential issues, such as mold or uneven curing. Patience is a virtue during this phase, as the extended curing period contributes to developing a more refined and well-rounded final product.

The benefits of proper drying and curing extend beyond flavor and aroma enhancement; they also contribute to the longevity and marketability of the cannabis product. Well-cured buds generally have a smoother smoke, reduced harshness, and a more appealing appearance. The consumer experience is enhanced, leading to increased satisfaction and brand loyalty. In the competitive cannabis market, where consumer preferences and discernment are on the rise, the quality of the final product is a crucial differentiator.

The importance of drying and curing methods becomes even more pronounced when considering the medical cannabis market. Patients seeking specific therapeutic effects often prioritize products with optimal cannabinoid and terpene profiles. Properly dried and cured cannabis can deliver a more consistent and predictable experience, meeting the needs of patients relying on cannabis for symptom relief or as part of their treatment regimen.

Beyond the consumer-centric benefits, adhering to proper drying and curing methods is integral to regulatory compliance. Regulatory authorities often impose strict standards regarding the moisture content, contaminants, and overall quality of cannabis products. Cultivators must meet or exceed these standards to ensure their products are deemed safe for consumption and satisfy the requirements of the evolving legal landscape surrounding cannabis.

While traditional drying and curing methods involve hanging and jar storage, some cultivators explore innovative approaches to achieve similar outcomes more efficiently. Commercial-scale cultivators may employ drying racks, automated climate-controlled drying rooms, or specialized curing equipment. These technologies aim to streamline the drying and curing processes while maintaining a focus on preserving the unique characteristics of the cannabis buds.

In conclusion, proper drying and curing methods are essential elements of the post-harvest process in cannabis cultivation, influencing the final product's overall quality, flavor, and market appeal. The careful control of environmental conditions during drying, followed by a meticulous curing process, allows cultivators to unlock the full potential of their harvested cannabis. The nuanced interplay between time, humidity, and cultivator expertise is integral to achieving a product that not only meets regulatory standards but also satisfies the discerning preferences of consumers and patients alike. As the cannabis industry continues to evolve, the emphasis on quality post-harvest practices will remain a cornerstone of successful cultivation endeavors

CHAPTER VIII

Maximizing Yields

Techniques for Increased Yield

Cannabis cultivators, whether operating on a small scale for personal use or on a commercial scale for the burgeoning legal market, often seek techniques to maximize yield and optimize their harvests. Increased yield not only boosts the economic viability of cannabis cultivation but also allows for more efficient resource utilization. Several techniques can be employed to enhance cannabis yields, encompassing various aspects of cultivation, from genetics and environmental controls to cultivation practices and advanced technologies.

Genetics plays a foundational role in determining a cannabis plant's potential yield. Selecting high-yielding strains with genetics geared towards robust growth, abundant bud development, and desirable cannabinoid and terpene profiles is a fundamental starting point. Cannabis breeders continually work on developing strains that exhibit not only impressive potency but also traits conducive to increased yields. Sativa-dominant strains, known for their taller stature and longer flowering times, may provide higher yields in specific environments, while Indica-dominant strains may offer quicker turnaround times.

Optimizing the cultivation environment is a critical factor in achieving increased yields. An ideal balance of light, temperature, humidity, and air circulation creates the conditions for vigorous growth and optimal bud development. Indoor cultivators often implement advanced lighting systems, such as high-intensity discharge (HID) lamps, light-emitting diodes (LEDs), or a combination, to ensure plants receive the necessary light intensity throughout the entire growth cycle. Controlling temperature and humidity levels within the recommended ranges for cannabis cultivation fosters a comfortable environment that promotes healthy plant development.

Utilizing the Sea of Green (SOG) and Screen of Green (SCROG) techniques are popular methods to maximize yields, especially indoors. SOG involves growing many smaller plants close together, aiming to create a dense and uniform canopy that maximizes light penetration. This technique capitalizes on the cannabis plant's natural tendency to produce a single dominant cola when grown near others. On the other hand, SCROG involves training plants horizontally under a screen or net, promoting an even canopy, and encouraging the development of multiple bud sites. Both methods aim to optimize light exposure and increase the number of flowering sites, ultimately boosting overall yield.

Employing the Screen of Green technique can also prove beneficial in outdoor cultivation. Outdoor growers can utilize trellises or nets to support the plants and create an even canopy. This method helps optimize light distribution, especially in regions with ample sunlight and encourages lateral growth, maximizing the number of potential bud sites.

Advanced cultivation practices, such as mainlining and defoliation, focus on shaping the plant's structure to enhance bud development. Mainlining involves pruning and training the plant to create a symmetrical structure with multiple main colas. This method maximizes the potential for even light distribution and increased bud sites. Defoliation, the selective removal of fan leaves during specific growth stages, helps direct energy towards developing bud sites and improves light penetration to lower branches. Both techniques require careful consideration and expertise to avoid stressing the plants excessively.

Nutrient management is a critical aspect of maximizing cannabis yields. It is essential to implement a well-balanced and tailored nutrient regimen that addresses the plant's needs throughout its life cycle. While nutrient requirements may vary during different growth stages, providing essential elements such as nitrogen, phosphorus, potassium, and micronutrients in appropriate ratios supports robust growth and bud development. Over-fertilization or under-fertilization can negatively impact yields and the overall health of the plants, underscoring the importance of precise nutrient management.

Cultivators have precise control over nutrient delivery in hydroponic and aeroponic cultivation systems, where plants receive nutrients directly in a water-based solution. These systems allow for optimal nutrient absorption and efficient nutrient utilization by the plants, potentially leading to increased yields. However, maintaining proper pH levels and nutrient concentrations is crucial to prevent nutrient imbalances and related issues.

In addition to traditional soil-based cultivation and hydroponics, some cultivators explore advanced growing mediums and techniques, such as coco coir, Rockwool, or deep-water culture (DWC). These alternatives offer specific advantages, such as improved aeration, nutrient retention, and water distribution, contributing to enhanced root health and overall plant vigor. The choice of growing medium is often influenced by cultivation goals, environmental factors, and the cultivator's expertise.

Supplemental techniques like foliar feeding, where nutrients are applied directly to the plant's leaves, can provide a quick nutrient boost during critical growth stages. However, cultivators should exercise caution with foliar feeding, ensuring proper dilution and application to prevent nutrient burn or other adverse effects. Foliar feeding is often utilized with root-based nutrient delivery methods for a comprehensive approach to nutrient management.

Implementing a well-designed and efficient irrigation system is pivotal in maximizing yields while conserving water and preventing nutrient runoff. Drip irrigation, soaker hoses, or automated irrigation systems help deliver water directly to the plant's root zones, ensuring optimal hydration and nutrient uptake. The irrigation frequency and duration should be tailored to the specific needs of the plants and environmental conditions, preventing overwatering or underwatering.

Pruning and training techniques, such as topping, super cropping, and low-stress training (LST), increase yields by manipulating the plant's growth and optimizing light exposure. Topping involves removing the apical meristem, or main stem tip, to encourage the development of multiple colas. Super cropping entails gently bending and stressing the stems to create a more horizontal canopy, promoting even bud development. LST involves tying down branches to open the plant and expose more bud sites to light. These techniques, when executed with precision, can result in a more robust and productive cannabis plant.

Technology integration into cultivation practices has become increasingly prevalent as cultivators explore innovative ways to optimize yields. Automated environmental control systems, equipped with sensors and monitoring devices, allow for real-time temperature, humidity, and light intensity adjustments. These systems enable cultivators to create and maintain optimal growing conditions, contributing to consistent and efficient cultivation.

Supplemental lightings, such as light-emitting diodes (LEDs) or extra high-pressure sodium (HPS) lamps, can extend the photoperiod and provide additional light during the flowering stage. This technique, known as light supplementation or light deprivation, allows cultivators to manipulate the plant's natural response to light cycles, potentially leading to faster growth and increased yields.

Carbon dioxide (CO_2) enrichment is another technology-driven approach to enhance cannabis yields. Increasing CO_2 levels in the cultivation environment during the vegetative and early flowering stages can stimulate photosynthesis and boost plant growth. However, proper monitoring and control are essential to prevent excessive CO_2 levels, which can harm plant health.

Cultivators may also explore using growth-promoting additives, microbial inoculants, and beneficial fungi to improve soil health and nutrient cycling. These biological enhancements can increase nutrient availability, root development, and plant vitality. Additionally, integrating organic and sustainable cultivation practices aligns with the growing demand for eco-friendly and ethically produced cannabis products.

In conclusion, maximizing cannabis yields involves a multifaceted approach encompassing genetics, environmental controls, cultivation practices, and integrating advanced technologies. Cultivators must carefully consider their chosen strains' specific needs and characteristics, optimize the growing environment, and implement precise cultivation techniques to achieve the desired results. The pursuit of increased yields is a dynamic and evolving aspect of cannabis cultivation, with cultivators continually refining their methods to meet market demands, regulatory standards, and cultivation goals. By combining expertise, innovation, and a commitment to sustainable practices, cultivators can unlock the full potential of their cannabis plants and contribute to the success of the rapidly expanding cannabis industry.

Pruning Strategies

Pruning is a fundamental horticultural practice in cannabis cultivation that involves selectively removing certain parts of the plant to influence its growth, shape, and overall health. Pruning strategies are employed for various purposes, including maximizing yields, enhancing light penetration, promoting airflow, and shaping the plant for optimal development. Cannabis plants respond well to strategic pruning techniques, and cultivators often integrate these practices into their cultivation plans to achieve specific goals throughout the plant's life cycle.

One of the primary pruning strategies in cannabis cultivation is the removal of unwanted or non-productive growth, commonly known as defoliation. Defoliation involves carefully removing fan leaves, especially those blocking light from reaching lower bud sites, to improve light penetration and distribution within the canopy. This practice is particularly beneficial in indoor cultivation, where maximizing the efficiency of artificial lighting is crucial. By selectively thinning out the foliage, cultivators can create a more even distribution of light, stimulating bud development in lower and interior sections of the plant.

Timing is crucial when implementing defoliation, typically performed during the vegetative stage or early in the flowering stage. This allows the plant to redirect its energy towards developing bud sites while minimizing stress during critical growth phases. However, cultivators should exercise caution not to overdo defoliation, as removing too many leaves can stress the plant and hinder its ability to photosynthesize effectively. Striking the right balance is critical to achieving the desired benefits without negatively impacting overall plant health.

Another pruning strategy involves shaping the plant's structure to optimize its exposure to light and air. Topping is a common technique where the apical meristem, or main stem tip, is removed to encourage the development of multiple main colas. This creates a bushier plant with numerous bud sites, maximizing the potential for higher yields. Topping is typically performed during the vegetative stage when the plant is actively growing and can recover more quickly from the pruning-induced stress.

Super cropping is another technique to manipulate the plant's structure and enhance light penetration. In super cropping, stems are gently bent or pinched to stress the plant and create a more horizontal canopy. This encourages lateral growth and the development of multiple bud sites, contributing to increased yields. Super cropping is often employed during the vegetative stage, and cultivators must exercise care to avoid causing excessive damage to the plant.

Low-stress training (LST) is a gentler approach to shaping plants and optimizing light exposure. In LST, branches are carefully tied down or bent to create a more open and even canopy. This technique is beneficial for indoor cultivation, where space may be limited, and light distribution is critical. LST increases bud development in multiple locations, creating a more productive and evenly shaped plant.

Scrogging, or the Screen of Green (SCROG) technique, involves using a screen or net to train the plant's branches horizontally. This creates an even canopy, with multiple bud sites exposed to light, resulting in a more uniform and productive plant. SCROG is commonly employed in indoor and outdoor cultivation, and the screen can be adjusted to accommodate the plant's growth.

Pruning strategies are more comprehensive than the vegetative stage, as some cultivators employ techniques during the flowering phase to further enhance yields. Removing unnecessary or tiny buds, commonly called "lollipopping," redirects the plant's energy toward developing more extensive and robust buds. This practice involves pruning the lower branches and tiny buds unlikely to reach maturity. Lollipopping improves airflow, reduces the risk of mold and pests, and concentrates the plant's energy on the most productive bud sites. Defoliation during the early flowering stage, often referred to as "schwazzing," is a more extreme pruning strategy gaining popularity in the cannabis cultivation community. Schwazzing involves removing most fan leaves and some sugar leaves during the first few weeks of flowering. Advocates of this technique argue that it allows for better light penetration, improved nutrient distribution, and increased bud development. However, it is a controversial practice, and cultivators should carefully assess its potential benefits and risks before implementing it.

Cultivators must tailor pruning strategies to their chosen strains' specific needs and characteristics, as different genetics respond differently to pruning practices. Additionally, environmental factors, such as humidity levels and airflow, play a crucial role in determining the success of pruning techniques. While pruning can contribute to increased yields and improved overall plant health, it requires a nuanced understanding of the plant's growth patterns and careful observation and adjustment throughout the cultivation cycle.

Proper pruning strategies go beyond the physical act of cutting or removing parts of the plant; they involve a holistic approach to shaping the plant and optimizing its overall structure. The goal is to create an environment that supports healthy growth, maximizes light exposure, and facilitates efficient nutrient uptake. Cultivators must be mindful of the plant's response to pruning and adapt their techniques based on its specific growth stage, environmental conditions, and overall cultivation goals.

The benefits of strategic pruning extend beyond yield optimization. Improved light penetration and airflow resulting from pruning practices contribute to the plant's overall health by reducing the risk of mold, mildew, and pest infestations. Well-ventilated canopies also create an environment less conducive to the proliferation of pathogens, supporting a more sustainable and disease-resistant cultivation operation.

Cultivators must approach pruning as a dynamic and evolving aspect of cultivation, understanding that each strain and growing environment may require unique adjustments. Experimentation and observation are critical components of refining pruning strategies, and cultivators often develop their techniques based on experience and a deep understanding of their specific cultivation parameters.

In conclusion, pruning strategies in cannabis cultivation are diverse and versatile, offering cultivators a range of techniques to shape plants, optimize yields, and promote overall health. From defoliation and shaping techniques like topping, super cropping, and LST to specialized strategies like SCROG and lollipopping, cultivators have a toolkit of options to tailor their approach to the unique characteristics of each strain and cultivation environment. Pruning is a dynamic practice that requires balancing maximizing productivity and ensuring the plant's well- being. By honing their pruning skills and adapting techniques to specific cultivation goals, cultivators can optimize yields, improve plant health, and contribute to the success of their cannabis cultivation endeavors.

Supplemental Nutrients and Boosters

Supplemental nutrients and boosters play a crucial role in cannabis cultivation, offering cultivators a means to enhance plant health, stimulate robust growth, and maximize yields. While the primary nutrients—nitrogen (N), phosphorus (P), and potassium (K)—are essential for cannabis plants, supplemental nutrients and boosters provide additional elements and compounds that can address specific needs at different stages of the plant's life cycle.

During the vegetative stage, cannabis plants require a balanced ratio of nitrogen to support vigorous vegetative growth. Cultivators rely on standard N-P-K (nitrogen, phosphorus, potassium) fertilizers to meet these basic nutritional needs. However, supplemental nutrients, such as micronutrients (iron, zinc, copper, manganese, boron, molybdenum), calcium, and magnesium, can prevent deficiencies and ensure optimal nutrient uptake. Micronutrients, in particular, are essential for various physiological processes, and deficiencies can manifest as discoloration, stunted growth, or other symptoms.

As cannabis plants transition to the flowering stage, their nutritional requirements change, with an increased need for phosphorus and potassium to support bud development. During this phase, some cultivators turn to bloom-specific fertilizers with higher phosphorus and potassium ratios. However, supplementing with additional nutrients like phosphorus-rich bat guano or potassium sulfate can provide an extra boost tailored to the plant's flowering demands.

Amino acids, the building blocks of proteins, are another category of supplemental nutrients that can benefit cannabis plants. These organic compounds play a crucial role in plant metabolism and the synthesis of proteins, enzymes, and hormones. Amino acid supplements enhance nutrient absorption, improve stress resistance, and contribute to overall plant vigor. Additionally, amino acids can be sourced from organic inputs such as fish hydrolysate or seaweed extracts, providing a natural and holistic approach to supplementation.

Plant hormones regulate plant growth and development, including auxins, cytokinins, gibberellins, and abscisic acid. Some cultivators incorporate synthetic or natural hormone-based supplements to manipulate specific aspects of plant physiology. For instance, auxin-based supplements may encourage root development, while cytokinin-rich formulations could promote cell division and lateral bud growth. Careful consideration and precise application of these supplements are essential, as improper use may lead to unintended consequences.

Mycorrhizal inoculants represent another category of supplements gaining popularity in cannabis cultivation. Mycorrhizal fungi form symbiotic relationships with plant roots, enhancing nutrient uptake, particularly phosphorus, and micronutrients while improving soil structure.

Mycorrhizal inoculants can contribute to healthier root systems, increased resistance to stress, and enhanced nutrient availability. Organic amendments like bone meal, kelp meal, or rock phosphate can also serve as slow-release sources of essential nutrients.

Bacterial inoculants, such as those containing beneficial strains of Bacillus spp., are utilized by some cultivators to promote soil health and protect against harmful pathogens. These bacteria can contribute to nutrient cycling, fix atmospheric nitrogen, and produce compounds that suppress pathogenic organisms. As with any supplement, understanding the specific needs of the cultivation environment and selecting the appropriate strains is crucial for achieving the desired outcomes.

Cannabis cultivators often turn to foliar feeding as a supplemental nutrient delivery method. Foliar sprays containing micronutrients, amino acids, vitamins, and even microbial inoculants can be applied directly to the leaves, providing a rapid nutrient boost. Foliar feeding is particularly effective during increased nutrient demand or when root uptake may be compromised. However, cultivators must exercise caution to avoid overapplication, which can lead to nutrient imbalances or leaf burn.

In addition to traditional fertilizers and supplements, some cultivators explore the benefits of organic inputs, such as compost teas or worm castings. These organic amendments contribute to soil fertility, microbial diversity, and structure. Compost teas, brewed from well-aged compost, can introduce beneficial microorganisms, enzymes, and organic matter to the soil, promoting a healthy and thriving microbial community.

As cannabis plants approach the late flowering stage, cultivators often seek ways to enhance bud development, flavor, and aroma. Phosphorus and potassium supplements, such as bat guano, bone meal, or specialized bloom boosters, are commonly used during this critical phase. These supplements maximize the plant's potential for producing large, dense, resinous buds. Additionally, some cultivators experiment with molasses or sugar-based supplements to provide an energy source for beneficial microorganisms in the soil, potentially enhancing nutrient availability and terpene production.

Terpene enhancers represent a specialized category of supplements designed to boost the production of terpenes, the aromatic compounds responsible for the distinct flavors and aromas of cannabis strains. These enhancers may contain specific compounds, such as myrcene, limonene, or terpinolene, intended to influence the plant's terpene profile. Cultivators interested in producing cannabis with unique and pronounced flavors may explore these supplements to tailor the sensory characteristics of their harvest.

While supplemental nutrients and boosters offer potential benefits, cultivators must approach their use with a discerning and informed perspective. Careful observation of plant responses, regular monitoring of nutrient levels, and adjustments based on specific cultivation goals are critical aspects of successful supplementation. Over-reliance on supplements or indiscriminate use without considering the plant's needs can lead to nutrient imbalances, phytotoxicity, or other undesirable outcomes.

Regulatory compliance is another factor that cultivators must consider when selecting and applying supplemental nutrients. In regions with legal cannabis cultivation, strict regulations may dictate permissible nutrient sources, application rates, and allowable ingredients. Cultivators should stay informed about local regulations and ensure their chosen supplements align with legal and industry standards.

In conclusion, supplemental nutrients and boosters represent valuable tools for cannabis cultivators seeking to optimize plant health, maximize yields, and enhance the overall quality of their harvests. From micronutrients and amino acids to mycorrhizal and bacterial inoculants, the range of available supplements allows cultivators to tailor their approach to the specific needs of their plants and cultivation environment. Thoughtful consideration, careful observation, and adherence to best practices are essential to harness the benefits of supplemental nutrients while maintaining the overall sustainability and health of the cannabis cultivation operation. As the industry continues to evolve, cultivators will likely explore new and innovative supplements to refine their cultivation techniques and contribute to the ongoing advancement of cannabis cultivation practices.

CHAPTER IX

Troubleshooting Common Issues

Addressing Nutrient Deficiencies

Addressing nutrient deficiencies is a critical aspect of successful cannabis cultivation, as the health and vitality of the plants directly correlate with their ability to produce robust yields and high-quality buds. Nutrient deficiencies can manifest in various ways, including discoloration of leaves, stunted growth, and diminished overall vigor. Cultivators must identify and remedy these deficiencies promptly to ensure optimal plant development and prevent potential crop loss.

One of the primary challenges in addressing nutrient deficiencies is accurately diagnosing the specific nutrient lacking in the plant. Common nutrient deficiencies in cannabis cultivation include nitrogen, phosphorus, potassium, magnesium, calcium, sulfur, iron, manganese, zinc, copper, and boron. Each nutrient plays a unique role in plant growth and development, and their absence or imbalance can lead to distinct symptoms.

Nitrogen deficiency, for example, often results in yellowing the lower leaves, starting from the tips and progressing toward the leaf base. This condition, chlorosis, signifies a lack of nitrogen for essential processes like photosynthesis and protein synthesis. Addressing nitrogen deficiencies typically involves providing a balanced fertilizer emphasizing nitrogen content through soil amendments or foliar applications.

Phosphorus deficiency manifests as dark green leaves with a purplish tint and can adversely impact flowering and bud development. Phosphorus is crucial for energy transfer within the plant and plays a significant role in forming flowers and seeds. Cultivators may address phosphorus deficiencies by incorporating phosphorus-rich fertilizers, bone meal, or other phosphorus sources into the soil or nutrient solution.

Potassium deficiencies can lead to symptoms such as yellowing leaf edges, brown spots, and weak stems. Potassium is essential for enzyme activation, water uptake, and plant structure. Addressing potassium deficiencies often involves supplementing with potassium-rich fertilizers, such as potash, to restore balance in the nutrient profile.

Magnesium deficiencies are characterized by yellowing between leaf veins, a condition known as interveinal chlorosis. Magnesium is a central component of the chlorophyll molecule and is crucial for photosynthesis. Cultivators can address magnesium deficiencies by applying magnesium sulfate (Epsom salt) or incorporating magnesium-containing fertilizers.

Calcium deficiencies may manifest as distorted or necrotic new growth, often associated with nutrient uptake issues. Calcium is essential for cell wall structure and overall plant integrity. Addressing calcium deficiencies involves applying calcium-containing amendments such as gypsum or lime to the soil.
Sulfur deficiencies can lead to yellowing of new growth and affect the plant's ability to produce proteins. Sulfur is a component of amino acids and vitamins, and addressing deficiencies may involve adding sulfur-containing fertilizers or amendments.

Micronutrient deficiencies, including iron, manganese, zinc, copper, and boron, can result in various symptoms depending on the nutrient lacking. Iron deficiency, for instance, leads to interveinal chlorosis with distinct green veins. Addressing micronutrient deficiencies often requires the application of chelated micronutrient solutions or soil amendments containing the deficient element.

Remediating nutrient deficiencies is not a one-size-fits-all approach, and cultivators must tailor their solutions based on the specific nutrient lacking and the severity of the deficiency. Soil testing, nutrient analysis, and careful observation of plant symptoms are essential diagnostic tools for cultivators to pinpoint the precise nutrient-related issues affecting their cannabis plants.

Beyond identifying nutrient deficiencies, cultivators must consider the underlying causes contributing to the nutrient imbalance. Factors such as pH levels, soil composition, and environmental conditions can influence plant nutrient availability and uptake. Regular monitoring of pH levels is crucial, as imbalances can affect the solubility of nutrients in the soil, leading to deficiencies or toxicities.

In addressing nutrient deficiencies, cultivators often employ corrective measures such as adjusting the pH of the soil or nutrient solution. Most nutrients are optimally absorbed by cannabis plants within a specific pH range, typically between 6.0 and 7.0. pH levels outside this range can limit nutrient availability, even if the nutrients are in the soil or solution. Soil amendments or pH-adjusting solutions may bring the pH within the appropriate range.

Organic cultivators may also turn to natural remedies to address nutrient deficiencies. Compost teas, organic fertilizers, and nutrient-rich amendments can enhance soil fertility and provide a slow-release source of essential nutrients. Cover cropping and crop rotation practices can contribute to soil health and nutrient cycling, reducing the risk of deficiencies over time.

Hydroponic and soilless cultivation systems require precise control over nutrient solutions, making it essential for cultivators to monitor nutrient concentrations and adjust formulations accordingly. Nutrient deficiencies can be quickly addressed in hydroponic systems by modifying the composition or concentration of the nutrient solution. Addressing nutrient deficiencies requires a proactive and attentive approach from cultivators, who must consistently monitor plant health, conduct regular soil or nutrient solution analyses, and respond promptly to emerging issues. Cultivators must also be mindful of the potential for nutrient excesses, as over-fertilization can lead to toxicity, nutrient lockout, and other adverse effects.

Cultivators can benefit from a preventative approach to nutrient management by implementing comprehensive feeding schedules, employing balanced fertilizers, and maintaining optimal growing conditions. Regular plant inspections, especially during critical growth stages, allow cultivators to detect nutrient deficiencies in their early stages and intervene before symptoms become severe.

In conclusion, addressing nutrient deficiencies is a fundamental aspect of successful cannabis cultivation, requiring a combination of diagnostic skills, corrective measures, and a thorough understanding of plant nutrition. Cultivators must identify the specific nutrient lacking and implement tailored solutions to restore plant health. By incorporating soil testing, nutrient analysis, and attentive monitoring into their cultivation practices, cultivators can mitigate the risk of nutrient deficiencies, optimize plant performance, and ultimately achieve bountiful and high-quality cannabis harvests.

Dealing with Pest Infestations

Dealing with pest infestations is an ongoing challenge for cannabis cultivators, requiring a multifaceted and vigilant approach to protect the health and vitality of the plants. Pests can range from small insects to larger animals, and their presence can jeopardize the entire cultivation operation if not addressed promptly and effectively. Cultivators must proactively implement preventive measures, closely monitor their plants, and employ targeted strategies to manage and mitigate pest infestations.

Prevention is the first line of defense against pest infestations in cannabis cultivation. Implementing a robust integrated pest management (IPM) plan is essential for creating an environment that minimizes the risk of pests establishing themselves in the cultivation area. IPM involves a combination of cultural, biological, and chemical control methods to maintain a balanced and healthy ecosystem. Cultivators may utilize companion planting, crop rotation, and the introduction of beneficial insects to disrupt pest life cycles and create an inhospitable environment for pests.

Companion planting involves strategically cultivating plants that deter pests or attract beneficial insects. For example, aromatic herbs like basil and mint can help repel certain pests, while flowers like marigolds may attract predators that feed harmful insects. Crop rotation, the practice of changing the location of crops each season, can disrupt the life cycles of soil-dwelling pests and reduce the buildup of pathogens in the soil.

Biological control methods involve introducing natural predators or parasites to manage pest populations. Ladybugs, predatory mites, and parasitic wasps are beneficial insects that can be employed to control common cannabis pests. These predators feed on harmful insects, preventing their numbers from reaching damaging levels. Cultivators may also introduce nematodes, microscopic organisms that prey on soil-dwelling pests like fungus gnats and root aphids.

Maintaining a clean and well-organized cultivation environment is crucial for preventing and managing pest infestations. Regularly removing plant debris, fallen leaves, and other organic matter can eliminate hiding places for pests and reduce the risk of disease. Proper sanitation practices include cleaning and sterilizing equipment, tools, and containers to prevent the spread of pathogens and pests.

Despite preventive measures, pest infestations may still occur, necessitating a rapid and targeted response. Monitoring plants closely for signs of pest damage or the presence of pests is a fundamental aspect of early detection. Common signs of pest infestations include discolored or damaged leaves, holes, webbing, and pests' presence. Cultivators should inspect both the upper and lower surfaces of leaves and the soil and growing medium to identify pests at various life stages.

Identification of the specific pest species is crucial for implementing effective control measures. Different pests require different strategies for eradication, and misidentification can lead to ineffective or harmful interventions. Magnifying lenses, sticky traps, and pest guides can aid in accurate identification.

Chemical control methods, including pesticides, insecticides, and miticides, may be used to respond to pest infestations. However, careful consideration must be given to the potential impact on plant health, the environment, and the safety of consumers. Cultivators should choose products approved for use on cannabis, adhere to recommended application rates, and follow withdrawal periods to ensure the absence of residual chemicals in the harvested product.

Organic and biopesticide options provide cultivators with alternatives to synthetic chemical controls. Neem oil, insecticidal soaps, and diatomaceous earth are natural products that can effectively manage certain pests while minimizing environmental impact. However, even organic pesticides should be used judiciously, as over-reliance can develop resistant pest populations.

Cultural control methods involve altering cultivation practices to disrupt pest life cycles or create unfavorable conditions for their development. For example, adjusting irrigation practices to maintain optimal soil moisture levels can deter certain pests, while employing proper spacing between plants can enhance air circulation and reduce the risk of fungal diseases. Cultivators may also implement physical barriers, such as row covers or netting, to protect plants from airborne pests like aphids or caterpillars.

Combining multiple methods for a comprehensive approach, integrated control strategies often prove the most effective in managing pest infestations. This holistic approach maximizes the benefits of preventive measures, biological controls, and targeted interventions while minimizing the reliance on chemical solutions. Cultivators can create a resilient and sustainable cultivation system by diversifying control methods.

Understanding the life cycle and behavior of specific pests is crucial for implementing control measures at their most vulnerable development stages. For instance, applying treatments during the early stages of an insect's life cycle may be more effective in disrupting its population growth. Additionally, rotating or alternating control methods can prevent pests from resisting specific treatments.

Pest management extends beyond the immediate cultivation area to the surrounding environment. Maintaining a buffer zone free of weeds and debris can help reduce the likelihood of pests migrating to the cannabis crop. Collaborating with neighboring cultivators to implement coordinated pest control measures can further enhance the effectiveness of pest management efforts.

Ongoing education and training for cultivation staff are essential to a successful pest management program. Cultivators should be familiar with their region's life cycles, behaviors, and identification of common pests. Training programs can empower staff to implement IPM practices, monitor plants effectively, and respond promptly to emerging pest issues. Regular communication and collaboration with pest management experts, extension services, or agricultural agencies can provide valuable insights and support for pest control efforts.

In conclusion, dealing with pest infestations in cannabis cultivation requires a comprehensive and proactive approach. Cultivators must prioritize preventive measures, implement effective monitoring practices, and be prepared to deploy a range of control methods when needed. Integrating cultural, biological, and targeted chemical controls, alongside ongoing education and collaboration, contributes to a resilient and sustainable pest management strategy. By staying vigilant and adaptable, cultivators can safeguard their crops, optimize plant health, and contribute to the overall success of the cannabis cultivation operation.

Solving Common Growth Problems

Solving common growth problems is an integral aspect of successful cannabis cultivation, requiring cultivators to be astute observers, proactive problem-solvers, and adept at identifying and addressing various issues that can affect plant health and development. Common growth problems can manifest as nutrient deficiencies, environmental stressors, diseases, pests, or other factors that hinder the cannabis plant's ability to thrive. To effectively manage these challenges, cultivators must be equipped with diverse knowledge, strategies, and hands-on skills to maintain optimal growing conditions and maximize yields.

Nutrient deficiencies are a frequent hurdle in cannabis cultivation, and their impact on plant growth can be substantial. Identifying the specific nutrient lacking in the plant is crucial for implementing targeted solutions. Nitrogen deficiencies often lead to yellowing of lower leaves, requiring the application of nitrogen-rich fertilizers. Phosphorus deficiencies can hinder flowering and bud development, necessitating the addition of phosphorus supplements. Addressing these deficiencies involves adjusting nutrient formulations, amending soil conditions, or implementing foliar feeding to provide a rapid nutrient boost.

Environmental stressors, such as improper temperature, humidity, or light levels, can profoundly affect cannabis growth. Excessive heat can lead to wilting, leaf curling, and diminished photosynthesis, while low temperatures can slow growth and increase susceptibility to diseases. Maintaining optimal environmental conditions through temperature and humidity control, proper ventilation, and appropriate lighting schedules is essential for preventing stress-related issues. In indoor cultivation, using climate control systems, fans, and supplemental lighting can help create a stable and favorable environment for plant growth.

Diseases represent a persistent threat to cannabis plants, with pathogens like fungi, bacteria, and viruses capable of causing various symptoms, including leaf spots, mold, and wilting. Fungal infections, such as powdery mildew and botrytis, can increase in high humidity conditions and poor air circulation. Implementing preventive measures, such as maintaining clean and sanitized growing environments, using disease-resistant strains, and applying fungicides when necessary, can help manage disease issues. Regular monitoring and prompt intervention are critical to prevent the spread of diseases and protect the overall health of the crop.

Pest infestations pose another common challenge in cannabis cultivation. Insects, mites, and other pests can cause damage to leaves, buds, and stems, affecting plant growth and reducing yields. Integrated pest management (IPM) strategies, including introducing beneficial insects, cultural practices, and targeted pesticide applications, are crucial for keeping pest populations in check. Regular inspections, using sticky traps, and early identification of pest issues enable cultivators to intervene promptly and minimize the impact on plant health.

Overwatering or underwatering are prevalent issues that can lead to root problems, nutrient imbalances, and poor nutrient uptake. Overwatering can cause root rot, nutrient leaching, and oxygen deprivation while underwatering can result in nutrient concentration, wilting, and stunted growth. Maintaining a proper watering schedule, allowing for adequate drainage, and monitoring soil moisture levels are essential to prevent water-related growth problems. Cultivators must balance providing sufficient water and allowing the growing medium to dry out between watering cycles.

Soil pH plays a pivotal role in nutrient availability, and imbalances can lead to nutrient deficiencies or toxicities. Cannabis plants generally thrive in a slightly acidic to neutral pH range of 6.0 to 7.0. Monitoring and adjusting soil pH as needed can ensure optimal nutrient uptake and prevent issues related to nutrient availability. pH testing kits or meters are valuable tools for cultivators to maintain a suitable pH range for their specific strains and growing conditions.

Improper pruning or training techniques can result in growth problems, affecting plant structure and yield potential. Incorrectly removing leaves, buds, or branches can stress the plant and hinder its ability to photosynthesize effectively. Pruning strategies, such as topping, super cropping, and low-stress training (LST), must be applied with precision and consideration for the plant's growth patterns. Overrunning or excessive training can lead to reduced yields and delayed flowering.

Genetic factors also contribute to growth problems, as different cannabis strains exhibit distinct growth patterns, resistances, and nutrient requirements. Understanding the characteristics of chosen strains, including their ideal growing conditions, flowering times, and potential challenges, allows cultivators to tailor their cultivation practices accordingly. Selecting well-suited strains to the local climate and cultivation environment can help mitigate growth problems and enhance overall success.

Excessive nutrient levels, often called nutrient burn, can result from overfertilization and negatively impact plant health. Symptoms include leaf tip burn, yellowing, and leaf cupping. Monitoring nutrient concentrations in soil or solution solutions, adhering to recommended application rates, and periodically flushing the growing medium can prevent nutrient burn. Balanced nutrient formulations that meet the specific needs of cannabis plants at different growth stages contribute to healthy growth without causing excesses.

Lighting issues, such as insufficient or excessive light, can significantly affect cannabis growth and development. Low light can lead to elongated stems, sparse foliage, and reduced yields. Conversely, extreme light, especially in indoor cultivation, can cause light stress and heat issues and affect overall plant health. Providing the appropriate light intensity and spectrum for each growth stage, optimizing fair distribution within the canopy, and addressing potential issues like light burn or shading are crucial for achieving robust and healthy plant growth.

Stress during the flowering stage can result in hermaphroditism, where female plants develop male flowers. This can lead to seed production and reduced bud quality. Avoiding unnecessary stressors, maintaining stable environmental conditions, and choosing stress- resistant strains contribute to a smooth transition into the flowering stage. Careful observation and prompt removal of any male flowers can prevent the risk of pollination and seed development.

In conclusion, solving common growth problems in cannabis cultivation requires a combination of knowledge, observation, and proactive measures. Cultivators must monitor their plants for signs of nutrient deficiencies, environmental stressors, diseases, pests, and other issues hindering growth. Implementing preventive measures, adjusting cultivation practices as needed, and responding promptly to emerging problems are critical components of successful problem-solving in cannabis cultivation. By understanding the unique needs of their plants, staying informed about best practices, and continually refining their cultivation techniques, cultivators can overcome common growth challenges and achieve healthy, vigorous, and high-yielding cannabis crops.

CHAPTER X

Cannabis and the Law

Overview of Cannabis Legalization

The landscape of cannabis legalization has undergone significant transformation in recent years, with a growing number of regions around the world reevaluating and revising their cannabis policies. Historically, cannabis has been subject to strict legal restrictions, often characterized by prohibition and criminalization. However, an evolving understanding of the plant's medicinal properties, changing societal attitudes, and a recognition of the potential economic benefits have fueled a global movement towards cannabis legalization and regulation.

In several countries, states, and regions, the legalization of cannabis has taken different forms, ranging from medical use to full recreational legalization. The primary distinction lies in the purposes for which cannabis can be legally cultivated, distributed, and consumed. Medical cannabis legalization typically allows for the use of cannabis for therapeutic purposes, subject to medical supervision and with specific conditions or qualifying medical conditions. Recreational legalization, on the other hand, permits adult use of cannabis for non-medical reasons, often subject to regulations regarding age restrictions, consumption locations, and permissible quantities.

Uruguay, in 2013, became the first country in the world to legalize recreational cannabis use for adults fully. This historic move marked a departure from traditional prohibitionist approaches and set a precedent for other nations to reconsider their cannabis policies. In the years following Uruguay's initiative, several jurisdictions, particularly in North America and Europe, have moved towards various forms of legalization, signaling a global shift in attitudes towards cannabis.

The United States has been a focal point in the evolving landscape of cannabis legalization. While cannabis remains illegal at the federal level, a growing number of states have opted to legalize cannabis for medical and recreational use. The state-by-state approach has resulted in a complex patchwork of cannabis laws, creating a situation where cannabis is legal in certain jurisdictions but illegal at the federal level. This legal dichotomy poses challenges for businesses operating in the cannabis industry as they navigate varying regulations and face restrictions related to banking, taxation, and interstate commerce.

Canada took a significant step towards cannabis legalization in 2018 when it became the first G7 nation to legalize recreational cannabis at the federal level. The Cannabis Act allowed for the possession, cultivation, and purchase of cannabis for recreational use, establishing a framework for the legal production and distribution of cannabis products. The move was driven by a desire to regulate the cannabis market, reduce the influence of the black market, and prioritize public health and safety.

Several European countries have also embraced cannabis legalization, albeit in different capacities. Medicinal cannabis programs have been established in countries like Germany, the United Kingdom, and the Netherlands, allowing patients access to cannabis-based medications under certain conditions. Portugal decriminalized the possession of all drugs, including cannabis, in 2001, focusing on a harm reduction approach that treats drug use as a public health issue rather than a criminal offense.

South American countries beyond Uruguay have explored alternative approaches to cannabis policies. In Colombia, for example, medical cannabis has been legalized, and the country has positioned itself as a significant player in the global cannabis market. Colombia's climate and geographical conditions make it an ideal location for cannabis cultivation, and the government's regulatory framework has attracted international investment.

In the Asia-Pacific region, attitudes towards cannabis legalization vary widely. Some countries, like Australia and New Zealand, have implemented medical cannabis programs to provide patients with access to cannabis-based treatments. However, the region, in general, has been more cautious about embracing full-scale recreational legalization.

The motivations behind cannabis legalization are multifaceted and often include considerations of public health, economic opportunities, social justice, and harm reduction. Proponents argue that regulating and taxing cannabis can generate revenue for governments, create jobs, and redirect resources away from prosecuting low-level drug offenses. Legalization is also seen as a means of reducing the influence of illicit markets, improving product safety through regulation, and addressing social justice concerns related to the disproportionate enforcement of cannabis laws.

On the other hand, opponents of cannabis legalization express concerns about potential health risks, especially for young and vulnerable populations. Some worry about the potential for increased cannabis use, impaired driving, and the long-term consequences of regular cannabis consumption. These debates highlight the complex interplay between public health considerations, individual liberties, and the societal impacts of cannabis legalization.

The evolving landscape of cannabis legalization has sparked conversations about social equity and justice within the cannabis industry. Many regions that have legalized cannabis are grappling with addressing the historical impacts of prohibition, which disproportionately affected marginalized communities. Efforts to rectify these historical injustices include expunging criminal records related to low-level cannabis offenses, reinvesting tax revenue from cannabis sales into impacted communities, and implementing policies to promote diversity and inclusion within the legal cannabis industry.

The legal cannabis industry itself has witnessed significant growth as more regions embrace legalization. This burgeoning industry encompasses various activities, from cultivation and processing to retail, research, and ancillary services. Entrepreneurs and investors have flocked to the cannabis sector, recognizing economic development and innovation potential.

Despite the progress made in cannabis legalization, challenges persist on both legal and social fronts. The lack of standardized regulations at the international level, varying degrees of acceptance, and the patchwork of legal frameworks within countries create complexities for businesses and consumers alike. The tension between federal and state or provincial laws in certain jurisdictions, as seen in the United States, adds complexity.

The global conversation around cannabis legalization continues to evolve, with ongoing debates, policy shifts, and societal attitudes shaping the trajectory of cannabis policies worldwide. As more regions grapple with the complexities of legalization, the importance of evidence-based approaches, public education, and thoughtful regulation becomes increasingly apparent. The journey towards cannabis legalization is not only a legal and regulatory challenge but also a societal evolution, reflecting changing perspectives on a plant that has been intertwined with human history for centuries.

Understanding Local Regulations

Understanding local regulations is a cornerstone for anyone involved in the cultivation, distribution, or consumption of cannabis. The legal landscape surrounding cannabis is intricate and multifaceted, with rules varying widely across different jurisdictions. Whether national, state, or municipal, local regulations dictate what is permissible or prohibited within a specific geographic area. The complexity arises from the interplay between jurisdictions that have embraced cannabis legalization and those that maintain stricter prohibitions. As such, stakeholders in the cannabis industry, including cultivators, retailers, and consumers, must navigate this regulatory maze to ensure compliance, avoid legal pitfalls, and contribute to the responsible and sustainable development of the cannabis sector.

On the international stage, cannabis regulations differ dramatically. Some countries have adopted progressive approaches, legalizing cannabis for medicinal and, in some cases, recreational use. In contrast, others staunchly adhere to stringent prohibitionist policies. For instance, Canada and Uruguay have legalized recreational cannabis at the national level, implementing comprehensive regulatory frameworks to govern cultivation, distribution, and consumption. Meanwhile, in countries like Japan and South Korea, cannabis remains strictly prohibited, with severe penalties for possession or cultivation.

Within countries that have embraced cannabis legalization, regulations often vary from one state or province to another. The United States exemplifies this regulatory diversity with its complex federal and state legal systems. While cannabis remains illegal at the national level, individual states have taken the initiative to craft their cannabis policies. Some states, like California and Colorado, have adopted expansive frameworks that permit both medical and recreational cannabis use. Others have opted for more conservative approaches, allowing only medical use or maintaining stricter prohibitions.

Understanding the nuances of local regulations is crucial for cannabis cultivators. Regulations typically cover various aspects of cultivation, including licensing requirements, permitted cultivation limits, security measures, and environmental considerations. For example, cultivators in legal jurisdictions may need to obtain specific licenses for cultivating cannabis, adhere to strict limits on the number of plants they can grow, implement security protocols to prevent diversion to the illicit market, and follow environmentally sustainable practices.

Retailers in the cannabis industry must also grapple with diverse and evolving regulations. Common regulatory considerations include licensing requirements, product labeling, advertising restrictions, and age verification protocols. In regions where recreational cannabis is legal, retailers face additional challenges related to the sale and marketing of cannabis products. Navigating these regulations is essential for ensuring the legal operation of cannabis dispensaries and promoting responsible retail practices.

Consumers, too, are impacted by local regulations. Age restrictions, possession limits, and restrictions on where cannabis can be consumed are standard regulatory features. Understanding and complying with these regulations is vital for consumers to avoid legal consequences and contribute to the normalization of responsible cannabis use. Additionally, awareness of rules surrounding product potency, labeling, and testing requirements empowers consumers to make informed choices about the cannabis products they purchase and consume.

Local regulations also play a significant role in shaping the emerging cannabis industry's social equity landscape. Some jurisdictions prioritize social equity programs as part of their cannabis regulations, aiming to rectify the historical impacts of prohibition on marginalized communities. These programs may include provisions for expunging criminal records related to cannabis offenses, reinvesting cannabis tax revenue into impacted communities, and fostering diversity and inclusion within the cannabis industry. Understanding and actively engaging with these aspects of local regulations is crucial for industry participants to contribute to the broader goals of social equity in cannabis.

The ever-evolving nature of cannabis regulations adds a layer of complexity for industry stakeholders. Regulatory frameworks are subject to frequent changes as lawmakers respond to evolving public sentiment, emerging scientific evidence, and the maturation of the cannabis industry. Staying informed about proposed regulatory changes, participating in public consultations, and engaging with advocacy efforts are vital for industry participants to shape the regulatory landscape and ensure that regulations align with the needs and aspirations of the cannabis community.

Local regulations are shaped not only by public health and safety considerations but also by economic and political factors. Governments often grapple with finding a balance between fostering a legal cannabis industry, generating tax revenue, and mitigating potential negative consequences. Striking this balance requires a nuanced understanding of the unique challenges and opportunities presented by the cannabis sector. Policymakers must navigate the complexities of regulating a historically stigmatized product subject to strict prohibition.

The enforcement of cannabis regulations also varies across jurisdictions. Some regions prioritize a cooperative and educative approach, working with industry stakeholders to ensure compliance and address issues proactively. In contrast, others may adopt a more punitive stance, imposing strict penalties for regulatory violations. The enforcement approach can significantly impact the dynamics of the cannabis industry and influence the level of trust and collaboration between regulators and industry participants.

For cannabis businesses operating in multiple jurisdictions, the compliance challenge becomes even more intricate. Each locality may have its rules, and companies must establish robust systems to navigate this regulatory patchwork. This includes developing comprehensive compliance protocols, investing in ongoing education and training for staff, and maintaining open lines of communication with local regulatory authorities. Collaborative efforts between industry associations, advocacy groups, and regulators can also contribute to developing coherent and effective regulatory frameworks.

Local regulations not only shape the legal framework for cannabis but also influence public perceptions and attitudes. Transparent and well-communicated rules can contribute to public trust in the legal cannabis industry, dispel myths and misinformation, and foster a positive image of responsible cannabis use. In contrast, poorly conceived or overly restrictive regulations may fuel skepticism and hinder the industry's ability to achieve broader social acceptance.

In conclusion, understanding local regulations is imperative for anyone in the cannabis industry. Whether cultivating, selling, or consuming cannabis, stakeholders must navigate a complex web of rules and guidelines that vary widely from one jurisdiction to another. The dynamic nature of cannabis regulations, coupled with ongoing efforts to address social equity concerns, underscores the need for active engagement, advocacy, and collaboration within the cannabis community. As the global conversation on cannabis continues to evolve, informed and participatory approaches to local regulations will play a pivotal role in shaping the future of the cannabis industry.

Responsible Cannabis Cultivation Practices

Responsible cannabis cultivation practices form the bedrock of a sustainable and ethical cannabis industry. As the global landscape of cannabis legalization expands, cultivators are accountable for ensuring their practices prioritize environmental stewardship, community well-being, and adherence to ethical standards. Responsible practices encompass many considerations beyond mere compliance with regulations, from cultivation methods to resource management. Cultivators are pivotal in shaping the industry's reputation and contributing to its long-term viability through a commitment to responsible cultivation.

Environmental sustainability is a crucial tenet of responsible cannabis cultivation. The ecological footprint of cannabis cultivation can be substantial, and conscientious cultivators seek to minimize their impact on ecosystems and natural resources. Outdoor cultivation, when feasible, harnesses the power of natural sunlight and reduces the need for energy-intensive indoor lighting. Implementing water conservation measures, such as drip irrigation and rainwater harvesting, helps mitigate the strain on local water supplies. Additionally, cultivators can adopt regenerative agriculture practices, such as cover cropping and composting, to improve soil health and reduce reliance on synthetic fertilizers.

Indoor cultivation, while providing control over environmental variables, often requires significant energy inputs. Responsible indoor cultivators invest in energy-efficient technologies, such as LED lighting and advanced HVAC systems, to minimize their carbon footprint. Utilizing renewable energy sources, like solar or wind power, further reduces the environmental impact of indoor cultivation facilities. Cultivators also explore innovative cooling and ventilation strategies to optimize energy efficiency and reduce overall resource consumption.

Beyond the environmental realm, responsible cultivation practices encompass ethical considerations related to labor, community engagement, and social impact. Cultivators should prioritize fair labor practices, ensuring workers are treated equitably and compensated fairly. Implementing workplace safety measures, training programs, and employee benefits contributes to a positive and supportive work environment. Community engagement involves cultivating positive relationships with neighboring communities, addressing concerns, and contributing to local initiatives for social development.

Social responsibility extends to addressing the historical impacts of cannabis prohibition, particularly on marginalized communities. Cultivators can actively support social equity programs, which aim to rectify historical injustices by reinvesting cannabis tax revenue into impacted communities, expunging cannabis-related criminal records, and promoting diversity within the cannabis industry. Collaborative efforts with local organizations, advocacy groups, and regulatory authorities contribute to the broader goals of social responsibility within the cannabis sector.

Responsible cultivation practices also prioritize product safety and quality. Cultivators implement rigorous testing protocols to ensure that cannabis products meet established safety standards for pesticides, contaminants, and potency. Transparency in labeling, including accurate information about cannabinoid content and potential allergens, enables consumers to make informed choices. Adopting good agricultural practices (GAP) and adhering to quality assurance standards further enhance the integrity of cannabis products, fostering consumer trust and confidence.

Water conservation and management are integral components of responsible cultivation practices. Cultivators must balance providing adequate plant hydration and minimizing water usage to reduce environmental impact. Drip irrigation systems, soil moisture sensors, and rainwater harvesting techniques contribute to efficient water use. Responsible cultivators actively monitor water consumption, implement water recycling systems, and explore innovative irrigation technologies to minimize their ecological footprint.

Pest management is another critical aspect of responsible cultivation. Integrated Pest Management (IPM) strategies prioritize environmentally friendly and sustainable approaches to pest control. Cultivators employ biological controls, such as predatory insects and beneficial nematodes, to manage pest populations without chemical pesticides. Regular monitoring of plants, early detection of pests, and using physical barriers contribute to a proactive and responsible approach to pest management.

Waste management practices underscore responsible cultivation efforts. Cannabis cultivation generates various forms of waste, including plant material, packaging, and cultivation byproducts. Responsible cultivators implement waste reduction strategies, such as composting organic waste and recycling packaging materials. Proper disposal of hazardous waste, such as unused pesticides or contaminated soil, follows established guidelines to prevent environmental contamination. Cultivators can explore partnerships with waste management services to ensure that waste is handled responsibly and in compliance with regulations.

Responsible cultivation practices extend to the ethical sourcing of inputs and materials. Cultivators prioritize sustainable and environmentally friendly options when selecting soil amendments, fertilizers, and other cultivation inputs. Choosing organic and locally sourced materials reduces the carbon footprint associated with transportation and supports sustainable agricultural practices. Responsible cultivators also consider their supply chain's social and ethical implications, avoiding inputs produced through exploitative labor practices or environmentally damaging processes.

Maintaining transparency and accountability is crucial for responsible cannabis cultivation. Cultivators should keep detailed records of cultivation practices, input usage, and testing results. This information not only aids in regulatory compliance but also demonstrates a commitment to accountability and responsible business practices. Open communication with regulatory authorities, consumers, and the community fosters a culture of transparency and trust within the cannabis industry.

Responsible cultivation practices also involve ongoing education and training for cultivation staff. Ensuring that employees are well-versed in sustainable cultivation methods, ethical considerations, and regulatory requirements contributes to a culture of responsibility within the cultivation operation. Regular training programs empower staff to stay informed about industry developments, adopt best practices, and adapt to evolving regulatory landscapes.

Technology plays a role in responsible cultivation, offering tools and innovations to enhance efficiency and sustainability. Cultivators leverage data analytics, automation, and precision agriculture technologies to optimize resource use, monitor plant health, and improve overall cultivation practices. Sustainable energy solutions, such as solar-powered facilities and energy-efficient HVAC systems, contribute to reducing the environmental impact of cultivation operations.

In conclusion, responsible cannabis cultivation practices are essential for the long-term sustainability and success of the cannabis industry. Cultivators bear a significant responsibility to minimize their environmental impact, prioritize ethical considerations, and contribute positively to the communities in which they operate. The evolving landscape of cannabis legalization emphasizes the importance of cultivating not only high-quality cannabis products but also a responsible and socially conscious industry. By embracing responsible cultivation practices, cultivators can play a pivotal role in shaping the future of the cannabis sector and fostering a positive and sustainable legacy for generations to come.

CONCLUSION

In conclusion, "Cultivate Cannabis Confidence - A Beginner's Guide to Successful Weed Growth" stands as a comprehensive and invaluable resource for individuals embarking on the journey of cannabis cultivation. This e-book not only demystifies the intricacies of growing cannabis but also empowers beginners with the knowledge and confidence needed to cultivate a successful and rewarding cannabis garden.

The e-book begins by laying a solid foundation, covering the fundamentals of cannabis, its various strains, and the legal landscape surrounding cultivation. It then seamlessly guides readers through the entire cultivation process, from selecting and germinating high-quality seeds to navigating the vegetative and flowering stages. Each step is clarified, offering practical insights and tips for novice cultivators.

What sets this guide apart is its attention to detail and emphasis on responsible cultivation practices. From creating the right conditions for healthy plant development to implementing eco-friendly and sustainable growing methods, the e-book promotes a holistic approach beyond mere technicalities. Ethical considerations, community engagement, and environmental responsibility are woven into the fabric of the guide, reflecting a commitment to fostering a positive impact on both individuals and the wider community.

The e-book also delves into the legal landscape, providing crucial insights into navigating regulations and legal challenges associated with home cultivation. It recognizes the importance of staying informed and compliant with local laws, contributing to a responsible and law-abiding cannabis cultivation community.

In essence, "Cultivate Cannabis Confidence" mentor's beginners, guiding them through the intricate world of cannabis cultivation while instilling a sense of responsibility and confidence. By combining technical knowledge with ethical considerations, this e-book not only equips beginners with the skills to grow their cannabis successfully but also encourages a mindset of sustainability, responsibility, and community engagement. As individuals venture into the exciting realm of cannabis cultivation, this guide stands as a trustworthy companion, providing the tools and insights needed for a flourishing and responsible cannabis-growing experience.

Thank you for buying and reading/ listening to our book. If you found this book useful/ helpful please take a few minutes and leave a review on the platform where you purchased our book. Your feedback matters greatly to us.